RELATIONSHIP
MATTERS

Kunlé Oyedeji

To Stephanie

Thank you for the love and support!
Stay blessed x

Kunlé

Dedication

I would like to dedicate this book to my Lord and Saviour, Jesus Christ.

"This is deep and timely. This is not just for young people, but for the pastors and leaders who want to understand what their young people face in the area of relationships."

Pastor Mary McCaulay

Pastor of De-Vine Sanctuary & National Teenage Coordinator of the Redeemed Christian Church of God

"I like the way the book covers each section and covers a lot of underlying issues in regards to relationships, along with the fact that it can even be used by an unsaved person. This book is a must for every young person."

Hafis Joel Raji

Dynamic Faith

"Kunlé Oyedeji is a leading Authority on Relationship Matters. His work and materials are outstanding and this book hits on the climax point of relationships that matter both for young people and adults. This is a must read for everyone that desires a happy home and a happy future."

Dayo Israel

Rehoboth & Make impact

"The language is down-to-earth, yet highly informative allowing the reader to get a true understanding on the concept of relationships. The book is practical, and almost has a 'how to' feel about it, which makes it digestible, practical and implemental."

Gbenga 'Minister G' Ajewole

Senior Minister Destiny Christian Fellowship & Co-Founder SAGE Ministries

"A great, practical and down to earth look at relationships......an enjoyable read"

Mark Liburd

Youth Pastor Ruach Ministries

"A fantastic representation for the extraordinary yet simple formula's used to solve the complexities of most common relationships"

Junior Crawford
Living Word

"This book is most needed among young adults who today find it difficult in dealing with relationships especially with the strong media exposure and wrong role models out there in the world. I commend Kunlé on touching on these issues at hand."

Iyabo Eferakoro
Youth Worker – New Wine Church: London

"Relationship Matters really brings the tools for successful relationships to the awareness of the reader. It is not overloaded with jargon but rather brings the basic truths about how to manage yourself and any relationship you have. It is insightful, practical and most of all effective".

Jackson Ogunyemi
Fixup Seminars

"This is not just a book on relationships, it's a manual for life."

Muyiwa Olarewaju
Riversongz & Presenter: Premier Christian Radio

"For me this book is the equivalent of scaffolding, enabling renovation to damaged and desecrated relationships, yet nursing adolescent relationships into a long-standing locale. A true prerequisite for existing and embryonic relationships"

Michael K. Ogunniyi
Out Of Zion UK.

Acknowledgments

First and foremost I want to thank my Lord and saviour the Lord Jesus Christ for the wisdom He has given to me to write this book.

I want to thank my dear mother a woman of God Grace Oyedeji forbringing me up in the ways of the Lord. Thank you for your endless love, encouragement and the time taken in proof reading this book. Thank you Dad and to my brothers Kola, Koye and Kunmi for believing in me, and for your encouragement. Special thanks to Koye for your support, and relentless work in correcting and editing this book. My love and thanks to Montré, Jennifer, my nephews Kiefer and Mayowa, and my nieces Aarinola, Ayoola and Alexis.

I am grateful to my Pastor and spiritual father Pastor Tayo Adeyemi for his advice, guidance and the time he took to edit this book despite his busy schedule. Thank you also to my Pastor's wife Mrs Adeyemi and to my leaders and mentors Minister Kola Taiwo, Brother Kayode Oluwaremi, Pastor Lori Hornback, Dave and Michelle Mahon, God bless you. Sister Iyabo Eferakoro and Pastor Kolade Adebayo-Oke (Chief), thank you for your listening ears and much appreciated support. I cannot help but mention my former Pastor and her husband, Pastors Lola and Tayo Oyebade for believing in me and encouraging me in ministry. I also thank God for the things I have learnt from spiritual leaders such as TD Jakes, Tunde Bakare, John Bevere and Joseph Prince.

Thanks to Raymond Peprah. Thank you for your love and support, thank you for opening your doors and resources to me with no restrain. Thanks go to New Wine Church, the New Wine Youth workers and New Wine Youth, I love and appreciate you.

Thanks also go to, Pastor Mary McCaulay, Pastor and Mrs Oyedele, Pastor Mark Liburd, Muyiwa Olarewaju, Brother Bukie Williams,

Blandine Nobime, Gbenga Ajewole, Tunji Ogunjimi, Dayo Israel, Michael K Ogunniyi, Bunmi Bello, Pastor Felix Makanjuola Jr, Pastor Akin Salami and Junior Crawford.

Thanks also go to Natasha Reid, Candice Mimi-Appiah, Emery Uwimana (DJ Mri), Will Twort, Daniel L Sydney (nMDi), Idowu Ilesanmi, Yemi, Sarah and the Adebambo family, thank you for all your support. Acknowledgements also go to, Aba Abekah-Mensah, Andrew Olaye, Andrew Williams, Chantal Bruce-McPherson, Dami Ogunleye, Dayo (Quadosh) Ayodele, Vanessa Addo-Yeboah, James Maduekeh, Yaw Ofe-Boakye, Jeanie Ebuzor (Instrument of Praise), Tobi Atunrase, Chima Ibemere, Yvonne Igunnma, Yetty and Taiwo Afolabi, Joshua & Caleb Ajitena, Kuda Thondhlana, Nimota Okunnu, Ola Akinlade, Tina Oshikoya, Marian Ogun. The Ojegba family, Jide and the Fishers, Uzo and Obi Durugo, Crystal and Helen Debrah. To Simply Andy, Guvna B, Triple O, Victizzle, Tunday, Prince and the New Direction crew and to all ministers too many to mention, keep up the great work for the Kingdom.

The last but by no means the least, I want to say a big thank you to my brothers in Christ Jackson Ogunyemi, and Hafis Joel Raji. I must say a special thanks to Alecia Hylton and special thanks to Ibiere Oruwari. What would I have done without your assistance? Special thanks to all the J4L team: Gerald Okullo, Muriel Lamin, Esther Towobola, and Bisola Oyedele. To the Kunlé Oyedeji Ministries team, Natalie Olarewaju, Celestina Olukoga, Adepeju Popoola, you guys are a great blessing to me. I love and appreciate you guys! Thank you for believing in me.

To those whose names may not be mentioned, you are not forgotten. Much love and appreciation...

Kunlé Oyedeji

Relationship Matters

If I had looked at my personal life to weigh whether I was qualified to write this book, you would not be reading this today. There are many people who will read this, whose materials await the shelves of many stores across the globe. However as a result of looking at their failures they question whether they are in a position to speak out. This trick of the enemy is designed to keep us down and to hinder the many who need our wisdom. The reason you have experienced what you have in your life to date, is because there is someone who needs what you have locked up on the inside of you. Be bold, be strong and do what God has called you to do. Now is the time.

Kunlé Oyedeji

Contents

Foreword

Relationships are vital to human existence. The fabric of our lives are woven by the network of our relationships. God said it all when He declared in Genesis 2:18; "It is not good that man should be alone". And I hope you know He wasn't just talking about marriage.

We are not solitary creatures – and God did not intend for anyone to succeed alone. There is no such thing as a self-made person. Everybody is somebody because of what they are connected to. Your associations will determine your destiny. When God wants to bless you, He sends someone into your life. But also, when the devil wants to destroy you, he sends someone into your life.

For all these reasons and more, we must never make light of our decisions to enter into relationships. And by far the most important of all relationships is the marital relationship. After your decision to accept Jesus as your Lord and Saviour, the most important decision you will ever make in life is the person you marry.

In *Relationship Matters*, Kunlé Oyedeji breaks down the subject of relationships into bite size and easy to grasp truths. He boldly takes on difficult aspects of the subject; and gives no nonsense counsel to people who are serious about building long-term relationships. As a young person himself and as someone who is passionately involved in youth ministry, he addresses young people with a candour that is difficult to dismiss.

Without a shadow of doubt, Kunlé qualifies to address young people about relationships. As his pastors, we have watched him mature – both in physical stature and in spiritual capacity. And he has clearly distinguished himself as a godly young man – a man after God's own heart.

Relationship Matters is not just another Christian cliché on relationships. It is pragmatic, it is down to earth; and it is in your face. It will challenge you to seriously evaluate your paradigms, re-examine your values and carefully weigh your decisions. If you ever intend to enter into a serious relationship, this book is for you.

Charles 'Tremendous' Jones said; "Five years from now, you will be exactly the same person, except for the books you read and the relationships you have". Well, you hold in your hands a good book that will help you develop good relationships. Get ready for transformation!

Tayo and Joke Adeyemi
Senior Pastors
New Wine Church, London

Introduction

I recall helping a young couple through a difficult period in their long-term relationship. As a result they recommended me to another person who in turn recommended me to another and so forth. I never understood why at that time until I had developed a keen interest in relationships. It is then that I started to ask myself why so many Christians were failing in preparing for a relationship, and matters pertaining to relationships. I asked myself why so many marriages were failing with statistics rocketing to amazing heights?

From my experience of holding a number of seminars, travelling and honouring multiples of speaking engagements, I believe that unsuccessful marriages have their roots in an unsuccessful understanding of a person and what relationships are supposed to be. A good marriage begins with a good friendship, followed by successful courting, righteous engagement and a Christ-like marriage. Relationships are never easy but worth fighting for in the long run.

Relationship Matters is a book for Christians aiming to give them helpful tips and profitable advice in regards to relationships. It is a guide and not a manual, as we are all aware that as unique as individuals are no books can determine human action down to minute detail.

I found that there are a number of texts that define what steps individuals should be taking when preparing for marriage. However I did not find a lot of writing for young people to turn to as a guide for preparing themselves for relationship commitment. *Relationship Matters* aims to fill this void.

The book is also a helpful pointer for those who are already in a relationship, and is packed with an overdose of principles, information, knowledge and experiences with the Word of God as its basis and source. I know you'll be blessed.

Kunlé Oyedeji

1. RELATIONSHIP MYTHS

Relationship Myths

I sat down one day and started to imagine what my perfect partner would be like. 5'11, and with an awesome figure sprang to mind at the time. The truth of the matter is that most of us can identify one stage in our lives where we took a few moments to imagine our perfect partner. Try it now. Imagine your perfect partner. How tall are they? What do they look like in appearance? Does he or she have stunning looks and a wonderful figure? Does he or she talk to you with such gentleness and words that sound like love songs? Good. Now you can wake up! I have a newsflash for you. Love is not as simple and as straightforward as the media may paint it. There is no perfect person or indeed perfect relationship for that matter. Each individual is unique and should be accepted for their differences. It is such differences that contribute to who they are. Understanding this reality enables us to set the premise for what we will be looking at over the course of this book, which is designed to help you have a Godly successful relationship, leading to marriage and lasting love. With this in mind let us first have a look at some common relationship myths:

Myth 1: 'If it is meant to be, it will be...'

Imagine I told you that I aspire to be the world's foremost basketball player. Imagine I told you that in order to do this I slouch around all day, I don't train or eat the right food, and in fact I don't even do anything other than watch basketball games on the television. Do you believe I'll become that great player? Obviously not. Likewise, people who believe that God is going to bring them that partner, and that all they have to do is sit around, and not want to date or put themselves in the right circles in order to enhance their chances of finding someone special, are also mistaken.

The Bible tells us in James 2:17 "Faith without works is dead!" To say that it is 'meant to be' without making significant steps towards a relationship is one of the reasons some continue to find themselves single. It is true to say as we will see later in the book, that when one is in the will of God for their life they are likely to find their spouse along the way. It is the duty however for individuals to be deemed approachable and to make themselves available to court those who they may deem as potential partners.

This same complacency also applies to couples that have begun a relationship and find themselves in difficulties. Your consistent contribution and persistence is required to allow the relationship to flourish. Nothing that is left in its original state has the progression of growth without being attended to. For example take a plant. A plant cannot grow by being watered once. It needs water, and the right conditions on a regular basis or its leaves will wither and die. A house that has been made clean can be left untouched for a period of time. However that will not prevent the dust from settling which will require the house to be cleaned again. When we stop contributing to our spiritual growth and our relationships the same principle applies. Relationships cannot rely on a long-term history to sustain them. It is down to both individuals concerned to make it grow.

Couples who have begun a relationship together were initially drawn to one another through attraction. It could've been a lustful attraction, or purely a heartfelt attraction. I believe that when you find someone that is attractive on the inside their outward appearance becomes increasingly attractive to you, as you are accepting them for themselves and looking beyond the physical. However two people are always brought together through attraction. If I feel that because 'it's meant to be it will be', and don't express an initial interest will it happen? "Faith without works is dead" (James 2:17). If either of you don't make a move you may both miss an opportunity. You have to be willing to take certain steps such as showing an interest when the time is right.

Myth 2: ' I don't need a man! / I don't need a woman!'
The Apostle Paul reminds us of a key element in the Word of God in 1 Corinthians 11:11. This is that men and women are not independent of each other in the Lord. Though in today's world some women thrive on being successful without a man in their life, we were made for one another. Men are looking for that helper according to the word of God in Genesis 2:18, where God tells us He will give man someone who is compatible and a help mate to them. The world paints us the picture that men and women are in competition with each other in a battle of the sexes. The world paints the picture that men and women are from two different planets with the use of Mars and Venus as metaphors. However we are warned not to conform to the world's way of thinking in Romans 2:12 and that's why the scripture in 1st Corinthians 11:11 emphasises that men and women are not independent from each other in the Lord and this view may be taken into consideration in our lives. Claiming an attitude of self-dependency needs to be balanced with the desire for compatibility with someone who can add to you that which will enhance your life.

Myth 3: 'There are no good men or women out there!'

I have often heard people say to me that they cannot find a suitable partner or I'll hear that 'there are no good men or women out there' either during a conversation or at the end of a seminar. However the bible tells us in Matthew 7:5 that we should first take the plank out of our own eye in order to see clearly (Paraphrased). That is to say that before we start complaining that there are no suitable partners out there, ask yourself: Are you a suitable individual for someone else?

If we all look at being suitable and compatible, accepting differences that come with relationships, then maybe there would be more suitable possibilities; bearing in mind we have established that there is no perfect partner. Each individual is unique and no one is perfect. However God has placed members of the opposite sex in our lives that are compatible with us. Therefore we have a choice in choosing someone that is compatible and allowing God to gel the relationship according to His will.

Myth 4: 'Opposites Attract'

Opposites can attract and can make good relationships. It is fair to note however that if opposites do attract, they must have agreed on something initially in order to cause the initial attraction, even if it was the fact that they are opposites that attracted them in the first place. So it is fair to say to some degree opposites sometimes do attract and sometimes they do not. God created variety, and variety is great. I advise people not to look to enter relationships in which the person is a carbon copy reflection of themselves. If you agree on everything, there would be no room for you to challenge one another and help each other grow mentally in some areas.

Myth 5: 'There is 'the one' out there for me'

This is one of the most common myths concerning relationships and marriage. Do you believe you have found the right one? Yet you are unsure? Isn't it funny how one can easily say that God said this and said that about other circumstances life may bring them, but might not be so sure when it comes to God telling them who they should enter into a relationship with, or who their husband or wife is to be?

Let's imagine a young lady named Lisa meets Tom and they intend to marry however unfortunately Lisa dies before they get married. Does that mean that Tom is not to marry again as his chosen one has died?

Some would argue that God would bring another woman into Tom's life. In this case let's say her name is Jane. Should this be the case then the question to ask may be why didn't God choose Jane first as Tom's chosen one before Lisa if they were both equally right for Tom and carried the same qualities? Why is it that Jane was only acceptable after Lisa had died? Why didn't Tom meet Jane before he met Lisa? Why would the apostle Paul make it clear that there are grounds for remarriage where one has been widowed if there is only 'one' person out there for every individual? In regards to the question of there being such thing as the 'one', it can become complicated. It is key to note however that the principle of there being one special person for us is not biblical but rather a Hollywood stereotype.

Christian psychologists have noted that this notion of there being one person on earth that is compatible with you is taken from Hollywood films where pictures are painted with the dramatic coming together of couples, suddenly meeting in an airport after not seeing each other for ten years. It would be unprofitable to assume that God gives man the choice of accepting salvation through Him as our free will, but gives more importance to who our spouse should be as opposed to where we spend eternity. Where we spend our eternity is more important than who we marry in the eyes of God. The word of God tells us in Proverbs 8:35 that he who finds God finds life. He, who finds a wife, finds a good thing (Proverbs 18:22). There is a significant difference between finding a good thing and finding life. So if there isn't one chosen person for us, what about God providing Eve for Adam? What about Isaac and Rebekah? Or even indeed Joseph and Mary? As this is a widely discussed topic let's look at this in much more detail.

Adam & Eve

A young lady once said to me that because God provided Eve for Adam, He would do the same in providing someone for us.

However what she didn't understand is that the original biblical text shows us that God presented Eve to Adam, but it was Adam's decision to choose Eve. If God made Eve as Adam's chosen partner then it would be fair to blame God for putting together a relationship which he knew Eve would cause Adam to fall and would end before it had even begun, as God is omniscient.

Joseph & Mary

In the Gospels' Joseph is encouraged by an angel to take Mary as his wife ahead of the birth of Jesus Christ. It is fair to say that God revealed to Joseph his wife to be and so therefore God chose Joseph's wife for him. We must remember though that God does not violate our choice of free will. Though Joseph was encouraged to take Mary as his wife he still could have opted out. Does that mean that Jesus wouldn't have been born and that which was prophesied by Isaiah in the Old Testament would not have come to past? Of course not. Had Joseph opted out God would have chosen another man who was willing to take Mary as his wife. God presents us with opportunities upon prayer, however it is our choice to choose with Spiritual guidance amongst many other factors from those He puts in our sphere as a potential partner.

Isaac & Rebekah

In the age of Isaac and Rebekah it was known to be the custom of the father to take up the responsibility of finding a wife for their son. This is what Abraham had undertaken with a view to wanting the best for his son Isaac. Let us look at the scripture in Genesis concerning this:

GENESIS 24: 1-9:

> *¹ Now Abraham was old, well advanced in age; and the LORD had blessed Abraham in all things. ² So Abraham said to the oldest servant of his house, who ruled over all that he had, "Please, put your hand under my thigh, ³ and I will make you swear by the LORD, the God of heaven and the God of the earth, that you will not take a wife for my son from the daughters of the Canaanites, among whom I dwell; ⁴ but you shall go to my country and to my family, and take a wife for my son Isaac."*
> *⁵ And the servant said to him, "Perhaps the woman will not be willing to follow me to this land. Must I take your son back to the land from which you came?"*
> *⁶ But Abraham said to him, "Beware that you do not take my son back there. ⁷ The LORD God of heaven, who took me from my father's house and from the land of my family, and who spoke to me and swore to me, saying, 'To your descendants I give this land,' He will send His angel before you, and you shall take a wife for my son from there. ⁸ And if the woman is not willing to follow you, then you will be released from this oath; only do not take my son back there." ⁹ So the servant put his hand under the thigh of Abraham his master, and swore to him concerning this matter.*

It is key to note here that Abraham was not specific in details with regard to finding a wife for Isaac but had warned that she should not be a Canaanite. Abraham had firstly limited the choice by claiming that the woman should not be a Canaanite and secondly should be from their kindred.

Abraham also recognised that though an angel would guide his servant this was no guarantee, as the servant and Abraham both came to the knowledge that the woman may not choose to be with Isaac, as highlighted in verse eight of Genesis chapter 24.

In reading to the end of the 24th chapter of Genesis we can see that the servant asks God to show him the 'chosen' one. As we read on to the end of the story we clearly see something interesting. The servant inquired of Rebekah for Isaac; Isaac did not choose himself and Laban and Bethuel both deemed this is of God yet they still allowed Rebekah the opportunity to 'choose' whether to go with them or not.

Upon arrival Isaac was told of that which had taken place, and yet he still also had a choice to marry Rebekah or not. It is with this that we see that we have the power to choose though we are to pray for divine guidance in such crucial matters. With this we can grasp the concept that there are a number of people that God has made who are compatible to us, and having prayed for God's guidance and speaking to counselors, your leaders and mentors, ask God to reveal such persons to you at the appropriate time. It is then your choice and you should not shy away from the responsibility, to find someone in that compatibility sphere and make a choice. The bible tells us in Proverbs 18:22 that he who finds a wife finds a good thing. That indicates that we are to do the finding. This can be a controversial issue amongst Christians, who may refuse to accept the idea that we choose who we want to marry based on God's guidance.

There are many discussions around relational myths such as we have covered. However the key above all is to wait on God. The key is to speak and listen to what God has to say to you individually in and amongst these discussions in order to find God's will for your life and someone who is right for you.

2. DATING, COURTSHIP, SINGLENESS & THE WHOLE LOT!

Dating, courtship, singleness & the whole lot
I have literally heard a number of individuals contest heated discussions about the terms Christians use in relationships. Debates such as whether we should use the terms boyfriend, girlfriend, partner, dating, courting and the like. In such forums I have seen the essence and nature of knowledge of such topics and relational matters being overlooked as a result. However should you still be unsure, let's have a look at some of the terms:

What is dating?
Dating is an old-fashioned word. Dating is simply known as when two individuals get together in order to spend time getting to know each other. It can also be referred to as when two are together in a relationship as boyfriend and girlfriend and see each other in this context. For the sake of this book I will refer to the term 'relationship' as when two individuals are together in a romantic relationship.

What is the difference between dating and courtship?

Courtship, in relation to the previous definition of dating, is where there has been a definite intention made known to the other person that you intend to share your future with them as husband and wife. As a result of this decision couples spend quality time together in a relationship before introducing their partners to family and friends and becoming officially engaged and then married. Christians prefer to use the term 'courting' even when they are in a relationship but are not officially engaged. Engagement followed by marriage is the final destination intended by both the man and woman when courting (Genesis 2:24). When there is no intention to eventually marry the person one is dating, the relationship seeks to have no purpose.

So why date?

Reasons for dating can include everything from being socially accepted, to being intimate with someone you intend to enter into a relationship with that will eventually lead to long-term companionship.

Some date in order to discover whether they share the same vision with another; whether they have common interest with a member of the opposite sex they could perhaps be with and one day marry. For others dating is to discover their likes and dislikes and to gain insight into the opposite sex and their behavioural patterns, as well as test the waters.

Some view dating as a necessary tool in relating to someone closely. It is an opportunity to find out how compatible they are with the person. Should you be contemplating dating, you must consider what is right and the correct way to go about it, seeking the appropriate counsel and taking the necessary steps (Proverbs 24:6): For by wise counsel you will wage your own war, and in a multitude of counselors there is safety.

Not everyone who dates does so with the right motives. Some date with the allure of the physical appearance of a person, and so hope to be with that person in order to satisfy lustful desires. Let us look into some of the notable differences between the male and female motives based on research I had undertaken prior to writing this book.

Male and Female perspectives

The physical appearance of a person plays a major role for a large number of males when they are seeking partners. In comparison to females, a female may be happy to accept the fact that a man is not the world's best looking guy, but has the necessary qualities in her eyes. However for most men today, in a sex driven society whether the female meets or has the attributes of a partner they require, they have to be physically attractive to be socially acceptable to them.

A number of reasons why males may tend to think with the wrong motives is because their first natural instincts are towards:

- Concern about the opinions of their male friends towards their partner's appearance.
- Sexual appeal to satisfy fleshy desires.

These are not correct methods or ways of thinking and should be avoided rather than used as a means for anyone to date or begin a relationship.

Wrong reasons to date:

Lust
Relationships that are based on lustful motives tend to fail. Christians should not act or think like the people of the world who look with a view to pleasing their lustful desires. We have heard the saying that

'looks do not matter.' However, general consensus will beg to differ in a contemporary society where 'image is everything'. Individuals desire partners that measure up to their own particular standards. What is it that will count when you grow old together if you start with lustful motives and ask yourself questions that focus on the physique of the person you intend to befriend? Their physical qualities or their heart? Looking for the true beauty within an individual is important as one day external beauty will fade. Looks are not enough in any case as they can be deceitful. Though looks are important and you should be with someone who you do find attractive. This shouldn't be the be all and end all in making a decision to be with someone.

To increase public image
Another reason why relationships tend to fail, especially common amongst young people, is because youngsters may tend to date on the basis of popularity. They may tend to date someone who is recognised amongst their circle of friendships or in their church in order to improve their own public image or to feel accepted. They may also choose to date because of loneliness or to gain materialistic items such as money, cars and other items.

Other reasons include peer pressure. The fact that someone dresses well or quotes scriptures from Genesis to Revelation without looking in their bible, and is recognised amongst individuals, does not mean that the person is right for you. An individual's popularity does not constitute as an acceptable reason for dating. If you find yourself interested in someone for such reasons as covered, ask God to help you and to change your motive to that of a sincere Godly one. There are a number of reasons why people choose to date in order to seek the fulfilment of certain needs. At times, people can become unaware of their motive to date. If you're interested in someone, pray and ask God to search your heart to see if it is true towards the individual.

Also listing a number of reasons for your interest may help you determine your true motives, which may have originally not been as clear.

Singleness

Some people prefer to remain single in life and would be happy living their lives as such. Singleness has its qualities. The reason why many might not see it as so is because of their concept of marriage. Some feel marriage is to take advantage of having sex, which is prohibited before marriage. With this a number of couples later find that marriage is more than just physical intimacy and reap the consequences of their wrong decisions. Married couples may tend to tell you that marriage is more than what it appears on the outside. Some may even tell you that they would have preferred to remain single for a longer period of time before getting married and some unfortunately may tell you they would've preferred to remain single altogether.

Practical advantages of singleness include freedom in terms of responsibilities that one may have if they were in a relationship. This is usually under- estimated. Singleness is a time of wholeness with God before being joined to someone as 'one,' should you choose to marry. A person should not be intimidated by the fact that they are single and should not follow what the world tells them.

Singleness in and out of a relationship

It is important for an individual to be 'whole' and emotionally complete while single to ensure that they are not entering into a relationship in order that their partner will make their incompleteness complete. In doing this individuals will find their weaknesses and their incompleteness rising to the brim of their relationship, which will in turn damage that relationship. This is why individuals find themselves hurting the very person they truly love, because they didn't know or understand the importance of entering a relationship as a whole and complete person in Christ, career wise, financially and emotionally. In order to take care of someone else in these key areas, it is important to be making significant growth and establishment in those very same areas of your personal life. I am not suggesting perfection, but rather attaining a level which is deemed appropriate by leadership, mentors and close friends who are an outside window into your life. They will help you to make a right judgement as to wether you are 'whole' and emotionally complete to enter into a relationship.

If you are currently in a relationship with someone and can identify with the fact that you are not whole but have been in what you or those close to you would class as a long-term relationship, ending the relationship is not necessarily the answer. Take responsibility for what you have and where your relationship currently lies without pointing the finger. Taking responsibility is the first step to reconciliation and restoration. The second step is to work on your singleness and ask your partner to be patient and support you appropriately in doing this. This does not mean that there will not be arguments and disagreements after this; in fact the opposite is very true. However the foundation for the relationship will be in the determination of working it out, knowing that this will only make the relationship stronger in most cases.

To leave a long term relationship based on your faults and mistakes can lead to losing out on what was actually the right relationship for you, if only you were determined to beat the statistics and work towards building yourself as a single person in order to have a successful relationship in the future. Learn from any mistakes, that you have identified that will not make you whole as a 'single person' and make a conscious effort to implement the correct attitude and decisions in your life and towards your partner with their help if they are willing. This will be made easier with the assistance of a personal mentor, and a mentor of the relationship, that's why it is important to have such people around you in your life, as no man or relationship should be in isolation.

Being patient as a single person

Ever heard the saying: 'everyone is doing it?' Remember that you are not everyone. Take note! Being a child of God makes you an individual and a unique person. The Bible tells us not to be conformed to the world (Romans 12:2). Do not look for what the world looks for. If you choose not to date as a young adult, don't let the enemy convince you that you are lonely because everyone is out on Valentines Day doing something with someone and you are not.

Being whole as an individual means taking responsibilities for your decisions, being emotionally stable, having a positive self-esteem and a vibrant and consistent relationship with God. Unless one is whole as a single person going into a relationship one shouldn't contemplate being with someone else, as there is a huge responsibility that goes along with it.

As a single person intending to go into a relationship or courtship, it is key to:

1) **Analyse yourself** questioning whether you are emotionally stable as an individual. This will help you to clarify whether you are entering a relationship for the right motives, if you are on the rebound or if you are looking for a relationship to fill a void. If one cannot recognise and understand their emotions how can they handle another person's feelings and emotions?

2) **Prepare yourself** this is one of the most important things you can do whilst being single and waiting for a relationship. If you fail to prepare, you prepare to fail.

Preparation time includes attending seminars, investing in materials such as books, tapes, and CDs that specialise on relationships and will help you prepare for this step.

Being single with a view to eventually getting married is a time to grow and mature in Christ and to study what truly makes a relationship work. Ask God to prepare you spiritually and mentally for this stage of your life when it approaches, should you want to be in a long term relationship.

This will prepare you for the responsibilities that come with relationships. The pruning must begin with you, and not with others. Before dating ask yourself these questions:

- Why do I feel the need to date now?
- Am I emotionally insecure? Am I lonely?
- Am I whole as a single person?

One must be whole and matured before one can consider a relationship or marriage. You need to be able to answer these questions honestly.

Deciding to date
If you choose to date look for qualities such as someone who will treasure you, support you, your goals and your dreams, respect you and most importantly choose someone who will enhance your relationship with God and not divert your attention away from Him. Likewise, as you're looking for such people remember someone else is also looking. In their search if they should come across you, would you match up to such requirements?

Dating unbelievers
According to the word of God Christians should not date unbelievers (2nd Corinthians 6:14-15). An unbeliever is someone who has not

accepted Jesus Christ as their personal Lord and Saviour through confession and belief, and does not live according to God's word and ways. In the same scripture (2nd Corinthians 6:14-15) the word of God tells us not to be unequally yoked with unbelievers. When people in Christ come together there is a bonding of light. However when a Christian and an unbeliever come together it is a bonding of light and darkness and therefore it becomes an unequal yoke. Let us take the example of a light switch in a dark room. When the light switch is on there is light in the room. When it is off there is darkness in the room. You cannot get a mixture of both light and darkness at the same time. It is either one or the other. Such analogy applied to Christian relationships equals uncertainty. Uncertainty is a negative word and tends to lead to a negative outcome.

Some Christians still find themselves dating unbelievers. While researching for this book, I asked some Christians their opinions on why Christians date unbelievers. Here are the results of some of my findings:

- Some stated it is a way in which carnal Christians could compromise and fulfil their lustful desires.

- Some said they find the physical appearance of unbelievers more appealing.

- Some said unbelievers appeal to them with material things such as money and cars.

These are just a few of the reasons as to why Christians may date unbelievers. A young lady once said to me on this matter that Christians dating unbelievers do not know that the enemy uses this as a tool to draw them away from God.

Some Christians believe that one day they could perhaps win their unsaved interest over to Christ and do not consider the dangers this carries. Winning them for Christ first and allowing them to initially grow in the Lord is the best approach. An unbeliever cannot offer you spiritual growth, which is the key to your life. The same scripture in 2 Corinthians 6:14 tells us that light cannot mix with darkness. Remember we are the light!

If you are dating - or even contemplating dating - an unsaved person you may believe that things will work out but bear in mind it cannot work in the purposes of God for your life! For example, your 'date' wants to have sex with you, but you don't believe in sex before marriage. Perhaps the guy wants to take you out to your favourite restaurant when you have got to go to prayer night. If that was a fellow brother or sister in Christ would you need to compromise or explain yourself? These are just simple examples of the negative results of dating unbelievers. What do you think they will add to your life? You can seek counsel from your church minister, youth leader or pastor regarding this issue. Whatever you do, remember the Word of God is principal, this is key to your life.

Another interesting reason mentioned as to why a Christian may date an unbeliever is that there are limited options available in their church. This is not an acceptable reason to date an unbeliever. There are many local churches and many members of the body of Christ. When you seek God with a pure heart He will put you in the right sphere at the right time in order to meet whoever he or she may be, along the path God has carved out for you.

I have noticed that in the Church some may have been brought up in the school of thought, which reminds us to treat each other as brothers and sisters, and to view each other in that way. In doing so some may find it difficult to view brethren in a romantic way. Some individuals may feel as if it is wrong in general, to have feelings for a brother or sister in that manner. That is why they may be reluctant to approach a brother or sister for a date in fear that they could be rejected and that such rejection could serve as a reminder each time they see, or try to relate to this person in church.

It was also stressed during my research that individuals feel as if they cannot be trusted to be alone with a fellow brother or sister without others speculating or questioning their motives. If you feel this way, it is important to find someone you can trust and speak to who will be able to advise you on how to approach this matter in a loving way.

Dating as a learning experience not a worldly concept

Dating, relationships or courting is not just for fun. It is something you consciously enter into when you're serious about getting to know someone with the view to beginning a relationship, which may lead to spending the rest of your life with that person. You should view your friendship and courtship with that end in mind. The world doesn't understand this and will tend to laugh at this view. They believe that you can date someone you don't intend to marry. What this does is bring confusion, unnecessary emotional pain and soul ties. They know one day it will end if there is no intention to marry the person and this sets them up for heartbreak and pain somewhere in the future because there was no underlying commitment to the other in the journey together. The world believes that it is okay to have a number of sexual partners at will. However each time a person sleeps with another person they give a part of their inner selves away as we will cover when we look at soul ties.

3. MATURITY IN RELATIONSHIPS

Maturity in relationships
Having seen a number of relationships fail and individuals go their separate ways, I had come to the understanding that relationship failure can be summarised in three categories.

Three reasons why relationships do not work:

1) **You are with the wrong person**
This is the basic and most straightforward reason as to why relationships do not work. This is when two people have nothing whatsoever in common and as a result it is impossible for the relationship to work.

2) **The wrong timing**
A relationship may not work if iniciated at the wrong time. For example this could be when the parties involved have crucial commitments to studies and therefore struggle to

find the time for that relationship at that stage of their life. It could also be where a person is emotionally attached to their past relationships or experiences and have created a barrier of fear ahead of a future relationship.

3) You are loving the person incorrectly
Another reason why relationships may not tend to work is because both you and your partner are not giving love in the way your partner would like to receive it. This can ultimately lead to frustration and a relational split. To avoid this couples would need to spend time exploring and discussing what they understand as affection and the act of love in an open and conducive environment.

This is my formula for relationships:

The wrong relationship + wrong timing = Disaster
The wrong relationship + good timing = Mistake
The right relationship + wrong timing = Hurt
The right relationship + good timing = SUCCESS!

Is God in your relationship?
Common excuses for people who find themselves with a challenge in their relationship are the words 'I suppose God's not in it' or 'It just isn't supposed to be'. The question is: How did God initially speak to you?

God is not a cruel God who has to wait for a disagreement or a relationship to end on bad terms before revealing to you whether it was supposed to be or not. Unfortunately it may have to end that way because we refuse to believe that the relationship can not be when God says so. This is usually the case when someone is emotionally attached to another person. The question is do we just rush into a relationship without firstly praying for God's guidance and speaking to others about it because of the dictations of our emotions?

When people say 'God isn't in it' I sometimes ask, why God didn't reveal this to them before hand if this was the case? One cannot blame every serious incident a relationship has to offer on God not being in it. Relationships are by no means plain surfing or an easy walk in the park! At times there will be major challenges, which will make the relationship stronger when resolved. However if one considers quitting on their partner at every disagreement the relationship will not be established on a firm foundation, and one could end up walking away from something that God was building on.

Infatuation is not a solid foundation for a relationship. One must make a decision to love through the thick and thin of a relationship. Also we must bear in mind that there is no such thing as a perfect relationship, and it is a lack of responsibility and maturity to pick the quick option out at every low point. Maturity, especially spiritual maturity is required before one can go into or consider a relationship. On top of this the most important thing is hearing God's word.

He will reveal to you and through Godly counsel as to whether someone may be the next best step for you or not at that stage of your life. Seeking advice is important in this, especially as emotions can cloud your mind and prevent you from hearing what God may or may not have spoken in these situations. This section is not to remove the fun in relationships, but to give you an insight into what also is in store in relationships apart from kisses and roses! So smile!

If you are finding it difficult hearing God's voice in general, then that should be your main concern and goal ahead of a relationship, as it is crucial to hear His voice in all aspects of life other than just relationships.

Perhaps you are in a relationship already or facing difficulties in dating leading towards this. If so ask yourself: Is this disagreement in my relationship about my character or choice of date? Remember that even if your choice is right it doesn't mean there can be no disagreement, it means that disagreements will not lead to a split. Here are some steps to help you grow spiritually as an individual and for your relationship:

Steps to personal and spiritual maturity:

Be a student of the word
In classrooms all across the country students are taught various lessons around a number of subjects. Have you ever wondered why two students can be in the same class, hear the same lesson but after the exam one achieves the maximum score and the other a failure result?

That's because one took what they heard, received it and applied it during the exam. Likewise it is not enough to just hear the word of God from the pulpit but to go back to our quiet place and study it further, delve into the scriptural references and meanings surrounding it, and focus on how you can apply it to your life:

> *James 1:22-25*
> *[22] But be doers of the word, and not hearers only, deceiving yourselves. [23] For if anyone is a hearer of the word and not a doer, he is like a man observing his natural face in a mirror; [24] for he observes himself, goes away, and immediately forgets what kind of man he was.*
>
> *[25] But he who looks into the perfect law of liberty and continues in it, and is not a forgetful hearer but a doer of the work, this one will be blessed in what he does."*

When you desire intimacy with God, He will reveal the plans and purposes for your life including matters pertaining to relationships.

Prayer

Prayer is conversation with God. Effective communication is two-way. Spend time building your relationship and intimacy with God in prayer. Set aside quiet time and a suitable place where you can converse with God and hear his word in season for you, as His voice in your life will overrule all factors. *1 Thessalonians 5:17: Pray without ceasing.*

Fellowship

God uses a number of means as well as prayer to speak to us. He may use mentors, leaders, and even friends to speak to us and to build us up. With this you must learn to put yourself in the right company with Godly people who you can be accountable to, build mutual trust with and fellowship with on a regular basis.

These are individuals who will uphold you in prayer and support you in love by any means they can:

> Proverbs 27:17: As iron sharpens iron, so a man sharpens the countenance of his friend.

Fasting

> Ezra 8:21
> [21] Then I proclaimed a fast there at the river of Ahava, that we might humble ourselves before our God, to seek from Him the right way for us and our little ones and all our possessions.

Fasting is not simply the denial of food, and there are various types of fasts that one can embark upon. However fasting is an opportunity for you to deny the flesh which wars against your spirit and consecrate yourself before God with time in His presence, in prayer and His word.

Fasting enables you to tap into another dimension of intimacy with God and causes your spirit to seek Him above. This enables you to achieve the supernatural, as you will see from the following example of Jesus:

> *Mark 9:*
> [23] *Jesus said to him, "If you can believe, all things are possible to him who believes."*
> [24] *Immediately the father of the child cried out and said with tears, "Lord, I believe; help my unbelief!"*
> [25] *When Jesus saw that the people came running together, He rebuked the unclean spirit, saying to it, "Deaf and dumb spirit, I command you, come out of him and enter him no more!"* [26] *Then the spirit cried out, convulsed him greatly, and came out of him. And he became as one dead, so that many said, "He is dead."* [27] *But Jesus took him by the hand and lifted him up, and he arose.*
> [28] *And when He had come into the house, His disciples asked Him privately, "Why could we not cast it out?"*
> [29] *So He said to them, "This kind can come out by nothing but prayer and fasting."*

4. TYPES OF RELATIONSHIPS THAT DO NOT WORK

Types of relationships that do not work

In addition to Spiritual growth and the importance of maturity in relationships, you may feel that your relationship is not progressing.

You may feel that the relationship is heading for an end in the near future though you are unsure of how and why. Should you want to clarify whether your relationship has the right foundation for a successful future, here are five types of relationships that do not work:

The unbalanced relationship

This is the type of relationship where most of the initiation, love and affection are displayed mostly by one of the couple. This individual is open and ready to commit to love whilst the other person is more uncertain of their feelings and their commitment. In such relationships where the love, communication and affection are not reciprocated between the couples there becomes an emotional strain on the relationship. Signs that your relationship may fall into this category include:

- You tend to call them much more than they call you.
- You tend to display physical and verbal affection much more than they do to you.
- You informed your family about the relationship and despite a significant time passing they haven't told theirs.
- You initiate most of the plans, such as dinner, evenings out and romantic occasions. Your partner shows little enthusiasm and hardly does likewise.
- You tend to initiate quality time and personal growth, however they become uncomfortable and seem less enthusiastic about it than you do.
- You tend to fit yourself into your partner's schedule, while they do not do the same.

The Potential Relationship

This is the type of relationship that is solely based on what the future may hold though there's no guarantee. Either one party or the couple are hoping that they'll have their ideal relationship when certain goals are achieved. This may include career or spiritual goals. As a result the couple stay together in hope that things may change for the better though there tends to be no progress and little change. They are in love with the potential of the person and not the actual person for themselves. They try to change each other to become like themselves and this only causes more pain. It is true to say that no relationship is perfect as mentioned in the opening chapters. However you cannot take someone to the altar to alter him or her. The behaviour displayed in dating tends to lead into courtship and in turn marriage. Hoping that a relationship in crisis will change once married is the wrong perception to carry. One must start as they mean to continue.

You have to play Hero

This is when one is in a relationship with someone who has serious physical, financial, or emotional challenges. Your partner frequently tends to feel inadequate, useless, helpless, depressed or overwhelmed in life. You then have to play the hero by calming this person down and consistently encouraging them, as they appear to lack self-motivation and low self-esteem. Leaving them would make you feel guilty, as you are concerned as to how they would progress without you because of their personal challenges. In this type of relationship one tends to play a parental role and tends to feel frustrated when their advice falls on deaf ears and their voice appears secondary to others. In such relationships one may feel obligated to be everything to their partner especially if they are coming from a background of relational failure. As a result one stays in the relationship convinced that no one understands such a person and could be of help to that person as they are.

In such scenarios one will continue to tolerate unacceptable behaviour from their partner and will be unable to receive true love from them as they rarely act like a source of strength for the emotional stable person. In such relationships one has to walk on eggshells to avoid hurting their partner and that partner believes that no one understands them. Such relationships are not profitable for any of the parties involved. This is why it is important for one to be whole ahead of a relationship physically, emotionally and financially. This is not to say that challenges will not occur where we will require the strength of our partner. However it is to say that we will not become over dependent on our partner and expect them to meet the needs God has designed for you to seek Him for in order to be whole and emotionally complete.

The inadequate partner

This is the type of relationship where a person with low self-esteem enters into a relationship with someone who has a high self-esteem. This type of relationship is also common where one places another on a pedestal. An example may be of a young lady who knows she has one or two challenges but has an interest in someone who is a minister or a youth pastor. She then views them with such a high regard as a result of their calling and is intimidated by them as a result of this and her internal challenges. She struggles to be open and real with this person and places extremely high standards on the minister or youth pastor in question, standards that he then has to live up to in order to feel accepted. In this type of relationship she may tend to go out of her way to show off to others that she is in a relationship with this person should they be popular to boost her own self-esteem. The inadequate partner often tends to do things because of what their partner thinks in order to keep them happy even if they feel or know it is wrong. Such people also tend to see themselves as "lucky" to have found such a wonderful person and never imagined achieving this. It is not the status that causes such challenges but rather the mindset one has created in looking to the other.

The Rebound

This is a relationship that emerges out of a previously broken relationship. It serves as emotional comfort and distraction from the emotional wounds and hurt that lies beneath a person's skin. Such relationships only fill a temporary void and are not built on a solid or Godly foundation. However no-one walks around with a label saying I am on the rebound or emotionally wounded, that's why one must be at a place of discernment and be in no rush to enter a relationship with someone, especially if it is off the back of a relational split. At times one may not be aware that they are on an emotional rebound, and may be longing to fulfill a lustful desire. As a result they would need to take some time out to question their motives for dating at that period in time. This will allow them to see if there are any correlations or expectations of their future relationships that are linked to that of their previous relationships.

5. GETTING PERSONAL

Do's and don'ts

True relationships are about what you can give not just what you can get. At times one can get hurt when a relationship doesn't meet up to one's expectations. So with this in mind what can you do whilst preparing yourself ahead of a future relationship?

Be yourself

For example, a boy finds a girl he really likes. There is an invitation to dinner. Their heart jumps with excitement, butterflies, pancakes and all!. "Where should I take her?" He thinks to himself. "What would she like?" He's convinced that he's got to make a good first impression.

One afternoon a young man came to seek my advice. He wanted to know of a good restaurant where he could take his date. Surprised at my response he smiled and asked me to be serious. I had told him to take her to a particular restaurant, which is not too expensive but rather moderate than to a plush restaurant he originally intended to go to in central London, which I knew he would not always be able to afford.

The worst thing you can do is not to be yourself when around someone you are interested in. Why should the young man in question take this young lady to a restaurant, which he cannot afford on a regular basis? That will be giving her a particular image of what he is not, and the impression that he can take her to such expensive restaurants on a regular basis. Don't give false impressions. Start how you mean to go on! If he did take her to the restaurant I had recommended and she had no qualms or complaints then it would be the first sign of acceptance for what he is able to offer her. It would show that she was interested *in him* and not where he could take her.

If he had taken her to the very expensive restaurant, she would probably expect a much more expensive restaurant or at least an equivalent on their next meeting rather than viewing expensive restaurants as a treat. Had it been the case the young man may have put an expectation in the life of the young lady that he couldn't live up to. This is a major reason behind relationship failure, especially among young people. They give the image of what they are not, and even get to the extent of borrowing items from friends and doing things such as compromising their standards and their identity in order to impress their dates. They pretend that they can afford to give expensive gifts to them that they cannot really afford. This is deception to yourself and to your date.

If you can be yourself and you notice an incredible difference in lifestyles and personalities from the person you are on a date with, don't fool yourself. Ask yourself after one or two dates if there is any potential for this to go further. False images and appearances will soon be revealed and will cause pain if you continue to put up an act.

Be who God created you to be! Be with someone who celebrates you for who you are and what you can offer them, not someone who tolerates you, or thrives on materialistic items as a foundation for their relationship.

Avoid mind games

Mind games are when a person decides to pretend to feel a way that they don't towards someone in order to hide their true feelings. This is done through means such as speech, body language and action. In reality no female wants to give the impression that she is an easy catch, and no man wants to reveal he is very emotional towards a female, as society paints this in negative light.

Remember one of our key scriptures throughout this book is in Romans 12:2 in which the word of God tells us not to be conformed to the world. To be conformed means to be similar to, or apply similar standards. We are in the world but not *of the world*. It is the world that tells you it is fine to play mind games and to cause confusion in the minds of those who interest you in order to give off, once again, a pathetic impression.

However we are not of the world. Ephesians 5:25 tells us to speak truthfully to one another, putting away lies, as we are members of one body. If two people are going to be together, they need to understand that there will need to be trust. Therefore they should sit themselves down and make a commitment not to play with each other's feelings and emotions. A relationship is made up of two individuals who make up a team and not opponents. If you or an individual are playing games you must question what the difference is between what you are doing compared to those of the world?

Mind games can lead to unnecessary emotional attachment, where there is no firm commitment to be with the person involved and that will lead to hurt, confusion and distraction.

Question your motive for dating

It is quite possible that one may think the feelings they have towards someone of the opposite sex is that of deep affection, when as mentioned earlier it could actually be the result of lust. I once read a book that was aimed at teenagers. It had a practical solution to whether one is in search of true love, or find themselves trapped in lust. The author looked at the scripture on love from 1 Corinthians chapter 13 verses 4-8, and asked the reader to compare their feelings with it, in order to reveal their true motives even if they were unaware of them.

Love is patient. Can you wait? Are you willing to be as patient as it takes in dating ahead of a relationship? If you are in a rush then something somewhere is lacking and this is wrong.

If you are concerned about losing the person you want to date to another person then that reflects their commitment to you and your insecurities. Before you date a person you need to be convinced that you are deemed serious in that person's eye. Love does not seek its own. What do you have to give in this relationship? Love is kind, but lust is critical and wants its own way without delay. If you are in a rush ask yourself why? Being honest about your motives and asking yourself questions are a true mark of wisdom and honesty.

Build on friendship

The best relationships are those derived from friendships where there isn't the thought of being together in mind. Ask yourself where you want to go with the relationship? Is this the type of person you could see yourself being married to? If not then why are you dating them in the first place? That means one day you'll have to experience the pain of breaking up. Treat your date the way you want to be treated. Be open to and honest with your date. Should you want to date and find that you are struggling emotionally, pray for self-control. Look to get to know the person well in different environments before making any crucial decisions. This is what I call the scouting stage in which, unbeknownst to them, a person's character is being examined. Dating can be more serious than one may assume. Once you have crossed the line of making your interest known it can be difficult to go back to the normal view of friendship in each other's eyes.

6. WHAT TO LOOK FOR IN A POTENTIAL PARTNER

What to look for in a potential partner
The word of God tells us in 1st Thessalonians 5:21 to test ALL things, or in some versions, all spirits. The verse goes on to say hold fast to that which is good. It is good to ask yourself what your motives for dating are, and whether they are genuine and to hold fast to someone who through being friends you can see has the following qualities:

Trustworthiness
It is important to seek and to see if a potential person is trustworthy. If, while in conversation the person you are interested in brings up someone else's person details for unnecessary reasons they may be breaking their trust. If it is a matter they could not discuss in their presence then it is gossip. If they can talk about someone else behind their back they can do the same about you. Indeed we all know the importance of trust. Trust will be a key foundation to any relationship, as there will be sides to you that people will not see until they get to a stage of closeness to you. It is important to be careful of whom

you allow to become close to your heart, and hence they have to be tested and proved trustworthy in your eyes. Relationships are built on trust between one another.

Attitude towards conflict

We all desire a compassionate caring partner. However relationships are not always as rosy. When difficulties arise, look for a person who is caring enough to sit down and sort out differences rather than walk away. Someone who is quick to respond to differences rather than get defensive because of your reactions to disagreements, someone who feels what you feel and will attempt to listen with understanding. Be quick to love, and slow to judge.

A compassionate person is someone with a genuine heart and cares about your well-being and will not turn their back on you in difficult times, or when your weaknesses appear on the surface. They are willing to sort out differences of opinion because of the genuine love they have towards you. These people are usually people who are known to be helpful and a good listener towards people. The key for all is to seek to understand their partner before being understood.

Compatibility

It is always helpful to be with someone who shares the same morals and sees things in a similar light to yourself. However we are all unique individuals and there will always be differences of opinion. You shouldn't necessarily be with someone who is just like you, as that may leave no room for growth. You may always see things the same and you may agree on everything. You wouldn't want to be with someone also who is trying to influence you to be like him or her. That would suggest that they are right in all they do. You have probably heard the saying that "you wouldn't want to be with someone who tries to change the person you are". Change is good if the change is of a positive nature. Some have a nature that cannot be completely changed. We all have weak spots that we ourselves cannot see. That is why we require people who can help us in these areas, and help us change and grow for our benefit. However there will always be a part of an individual that cannot be changed, as that's who they are. Look for someone who compliments your lifestyle, not someone who flatters you with sweet words but someone who will tell you the truth; even though those words may hurt they will be helpful. The word of God tells us in Proverbs 27:6 that the wounds of a friend can be trusted, but an enemy multiplies kisses. People who are not true to you flatter to keep you happy. True friends want to see you improve and grow and so will tell you the truth for your own good. Avoid dating someone who doesn't contribute anything to you or doesn't push you in the right direction, which is towards God and your dreams.

Someone that supports your vision

You want to be with someone that will support your dreams and visions. Someone who will encourage you to walk the walk through thick and thin, through happiness, sadness, tears and joy. Someone who puts God before you. Someone with common interests would be helpful but this isn't a must in every case. I remember a young lady who showed an interest in me as a person but not in my vision. I knew that I needed to be with someone who, when I come home from ministry work would be able to pray and support me in what it is that I do. So I knew that it wouldn't work and spared both of us of any potential difficulty before becoming emotionally attached.

Being attracted to someone is not a good enough foundation on its own. You need someone who is ready to accept your lifestyle and support you, your vision and ministry along the way.

You can seek such potentials by looking at how they behave towards you in your scouting stage.

God centred

We've already established that your date should be a Christian. Now we are talking about someone who is totally God focused. When they put God first your relationship will thrive. If God is not the first in their life you will soon become an idol, and God may take that person from you, as He doesn't want anything taking His rightful place in your life. This is the reason why some people don't have peace in their relationships. Not because it isn't right, but unknowingly it has become an idol. Things such as their quiet time before God have been replaced with long phone calls to their partner and there is no balance. If God is first in someone's life it will reflect in his or her lifestyle, personality, character and speech.

Remember going to church doesn't make you a Christian just as sleeping in a garage doesn't make you a car! So look for true character, as that's what makes or breaks a person. That's why it's best to scout first before following through. Look for someone who can build you up and challenge you to believe in what you do and want to achieve, and make this person someone who you can do the very same things for.

Matthew 7: 16: *You will know them by their fruits.*

Remember that love is about giving not just taking. When this person has God first they will demonstrate God's love for you and will be filled with not your love first, but God's love. Now who wouldn't want to be married to someone who is filled with the love of God and the Holy Spirit? Someone who will provide a forum to study the word and pray together. If the focus of your relationship is just feasting on meals and visiting the cinema, then you may be building your relationship on the wrong foundation and it may not survive the storms and challenges that relationships ultimately face. There needs to be the right balance and your potential partner needs to be able to demonstrate this. The

56

relationship that stands is that which is built on the rock, which is God and His word.

> *Luke 6:*
> [46]*"Why do you call me, 'Lord, Lord,' and do not do what I say?* [47] *I will show you what he is like who comes to me and hears my words and puts them into practice.* [48]*He is like a man building a house, who dug down deep and laid the foundation on rock. When a flood came, the torrent struck that house but could not shake it, because it was well built.* [49]*But the one who hears my words and does not put them into practice is like a man who built a house on the ground without a foundation. The moment the torrent struck that house, it collapsed and its destruction was complete."*

Ladies reading this are probably wondering 'there is no boy or man out there like that! They are all the same!' While the men are thinking: 'I don't think you'll find a lady like that - they don't know what they want'. However, rather than complaining that there are not enough like-minded men or women with such qualities why don't you aim to become that type of person? The word of God tells us in Luke 6:

> [41]*"Why do you look at the speck of sawdust in your brother's eye and pay no attention to the plank in your own eye?* [42]*How can you say to your brother, 'Brother, let me take the speck out of your eye,' when you yourself fail to see the plank in your own eye? You hypocrite, first take the plank out of your eye, and then you will see clearly to remove the speck from your brother's eye."*

Start with brotherly love, which is the love God commands. This is the love between brothers and sisters in Christ. Communication that is clear and specific helps even in the most difficult situations. With the right behaviour and attitude we'll all have many like-minded people around us to enter relationships with. Start with yourself; look at how you can improve. Ask yourself what kind of a partner you would be if you were in a relationship. With the right behaviour and attitude we'll focus more on God, building one another up in Christ, having humble, compassionate, caring and loving God-fearing partners. We will have good and godly relationships, learn a lot and benefit from one another a great deal.

Emotional Openness

The essence of a relationship is to confide in one another creating emotional intimacy. This is why it is important to see how trustworthy one is during your dating period. Somebody who is not willing to open up is not ready for a relationship and should continue at a friendship level until they are ready to share their deepest fears, and thoughts in a committed relationship.

Commitment to personal growth

It is crucial to be a person who is committed to personal growth and to be in a relationship with someone who has that same commitment. Where this commitment is only upheld by one person the growth of the relationship will not be aided. A commitment to personal growth demonstrates the intention to grow in learning about relationships ahead of courting and in marriage. This once again signifies the intention to become a better person for your partner. Personal growth means investing in books and materials as well as attending seminars and discussing aspects of your relationship that need improving and how to go about making such adjustments.

Good Self-esteem

Look to be with someone who has good self-esteem. This is a person who is a self-motivator, knows how to take responsibility for their actions and doesn't wallow in self-pity. Being in a relationship where one has a low self-esteem can harm the relationship. There will be an over reliance on the partner to give additional emotional support and this will cause a strain on your relationship in the long term.

Positive Attitude

This follows on from having a good self-esteem. It is important to have a good attitude in life, as your attitude determines your altitude. A good attitude is crucial to how one views their relationship during difficult circumstances, in the long term as well as in its development as a whole. People with low self-esteem tend to carry negative attitudes and focus on the worst aspects of every situation.

Integrity

How do they treat others? Do they give tips to reward the excellence of the people they come into contact with? Do they have key morals they will not compromise on? How do friends, family and fellow brothers and sisters in the faith view and speak of them? These are all clues that give us an indication of one's integrity.

7. RELATIONSHIP ROLE MODELS

The Story and character of Ruth

In the book of Ruth we have a story where Ruth and Orpah have lost their husbands and are left with their mother-in-law Naomi. She has also lost her husband as well as her two sons. You can imagine the pain that Naomi also must have experienced. Naomi encourages both women to return to their mothers' houses, as she has no more sons for them to re-marry. Orpah decides to leave while Ruth chooses to remain with Naomi. What can we learn from this? Though Ruth had lost her husband, she was able to look beyond her own pain to that of her mother-in-law's. Every guy wants a woman or a young lady that will stick by him in the most difficult times. Ruth displayed such character in doing just this. Relationships will face challenges; the strongest ones are those that prevail through such times. It is easy to be faithful when all is well. However Ruth wanted to be there for Naomi regardless of whether things were going well or not. Though she was mourning the loss of her own husband Orpah was not able to see beyond her own pain in order to reach out to others. I have witnessed some females behave in this manner. When they get hurt or when challenges arise, they want to end the relationship or walk away from it, as opposed to fighting for that relationship.

Ruth wasn't lazy. She went out to work, so that she might be recognised. She wasn't the type of lady who sat around waiting for "Superman" to drop out of heaven. She wasn't waiting for that guy to come along and pay the mortgage for the house she was to live in. She knew that if she was going to achieve anything in life she would put her hands to work for it inspite of her circumstances. A Godly woman is someone who works hard in order to bring something to the table to offer a potential partner as opposed to someone who expects the man to do everything.

In the book of Ruth chapter 2:11 Ruth had found favour in the eyes of Boaz. This is because all that she had done for her mother-in-law Naomi had been reported. What did Ruth do? She left her home, put aside her own agenda in order to be faithful and stick by Naomi. That is an act of character. Her hard work, loyalty and faithfulness in tough times were reflected in her character and was recognised by Boaz who in turn favoured her. We go on to see in chapter 3:10 something key in the amazing character of Ruth. Boaz compliments Ruth on the fact that she has shown more kindness in the end than in the beginning. This is to say that as things got tougher she became more of a giver and her faith increased. Ruth's heart wasn't focused on the finances of Boaz. A true woman doesn't enter a relationship because of the material things a man may have. A true woman of God looks beyond perishable items such as cars and even wealth to see the heart, vision, lifestyle and spirituality of a man, as this is what the relationship will live by. To solely want to be with someone because of what they have and not who they are is not godly or a display of Christ like character.

All of Ruth's actions were based upon a pure heart and this led to her being recognised as a virtuous woman amongst all the people of her city. A woman of true character like Ruth doesn't have to speak of her own good. Wherever there is amazing character people will recognise this in you.

These are characteristics of a Godly woman based upon a great example in the life of Ruth. As a young lady who may consider entering into a relationship, ask yourself whether you can be like Ruth, and hence be a helper to your partner and a woman of excellent character.

The story and character of Joseph

Before Eve, Adam had responsibility. A man of God is a man who has a dream. He doesn't blame society for where he is today, but takes responsibility and is determined to make the most out of what he has while on the way to where he wants to be. Today's generation needs more young men who have a passion and drive to achieve amazing dreams. Not men who lack perseverance and are easily susceptible to peer pressure. This wasn't the case of Joseph. His dream took a while to come to pass, but nothing was going to put him off, not even his own family disowning him. The ultimate characteristic of a real man is faithfulness. Joseph's true character and faithfulness to God's word are demonstrated in Genesis Chapter 39:6-21. Joseph could have slept with Potiphar's wife and possibly got away with it as there was no one else there to witness it. Joseph however feared God, not man. He knew that doing this would be wrong. So he remained faithful to God though Potiphar's wife tempted him and cast eyes upon him in order to get him to lie with her. Joseph fled. A man of God recognises where and when to flee ahead of time, in order to be faithful to God and if they are already in a relationship, their partner.

In Genesis 40, Joseph recognised that as a son of God he had access to that which belonged to the Lord. He was able to go on to interpret dreams for others. He was helpful to others and he was a problem solver. In life we either create problems or solve problems. The characteristic of a Godly man is someone who can bring solutions to unanswered questions and complete a Godly woman through a relationship with Christ. He is able to offer these aforementioned attributes to a potential partner and is seen as an addition not a subtraction.

There is a saying that marriage is the union of two forgivers. It is generally the ego of men to prove themselves right and justify their actions. Men tend to think logically. For some men who are yet to have attained a level of maturity, if they are attacked they want to come back stronger to prove that they deserve to be on top or that they are right. Despite what Joseph's family had done to him, he was still willing to forgive, love and accept them once again. A Godly man understands that a potential partner and those around them can hurt them at times, however they are still willing to extend an arm of love as opposed to retaliation. Forgiveness and letting go of past issues can be hard, but more importantly the good news is that it can be achieved. If you are struggling with forgiveness ask God to help you right now. It could be holding you back from releasing you to enter or pursue a relationship that is right for you.

We must also understand that Joseph was a successful and responsible man as seen in the Word of God. A man of God is responsible for their actions and what they do. In order to become the leaders God ordained for us to be in a society that tends to lack a presence of real men, we are to do as Christ did as opposed to blaming others or looking to them for excuses.

8. HOW TO PREPARE FOR A RELATIONSHIP

Put friendship first

Single people are marketing people, always putting on their best face and displaying the best side of themselves in the interest of others. Once a person knows you are interested in them it is unlikely that they will fully be themselves around you. The best relationships are friendships that started without romantic intentions. These friendships allow people to look at one another without any emotional attachment to cloud their judgement. If you're interested in a person, be a friend to that person. See what their interests are, and their views are on key areas such as church, family, relationships, finance, spirituality and life. Doing this in a non-threatening way requires effective communication skills. It means learning how to ask the right questions in order to gain the right information. It means involving yourself in their circle of friends to see how you get on with them and how they are in various circumstances. Would that guy usually hold the door open for you when you leave the restaurant? Well if he is smart and he knows that the female is interested he would try to impress her with his gentlemanly mannerisms. However if he didn't know the lady was interested would he still do the same? His true mannerisms would be revealed. Use this method to find out who the person really is that you are interested in.

Commit to self development
People often spend time praying for God to bring that special person into their life. However the problem arises when God brings us that individual, and we forget to pray: 'Lord prepare me for that special person when they finally arrive.'

> *Proverbs 1:5 says: 'A wise man will hear and increase learning, and a man of understanding will attain wise counsel...'.*

It's amazing that one will spend a great deal of time in education studying ahead of a career or for a job, but will spend relatively little time to learn and study about relationships and marriage which is supposed to last until death. Learning to understand the differences between the behavioural and thought patterns of each sex, along with reading relationship books and attending seminars will enhance your relationship. The problem is people spend relatively little time doing this. They find themselves stuck in situations which they would have been better prepared for if only they had attended a seminar or two, talked to married couples and mentors. Develop yourself as a person who both mentally, and spiritually is able to bring something to the table to offer a potential partner, not just in relationships but also in all areas of life.

Know what you want
Imagine the manager of a soccer club, telling his chairman he wants to buy a player for his team. The chairman responds by asking him whether he would like to purchase a goalkeeper, defender, midfielder or attacker. The manager responds: 'I don't know.'

It would appear that the manager either wants to add a player to his squad for reasons, which are unimportant, or he hasn't analysed his squad properly. Not every soccer player who is available for transfer will appeal to this manager, he is interested in those who are capable of adding a dimension to his team. So what can we learn from this? As an individual you need to know what you require in a partner, and this goes beyond external appearance and materialism.

You need to be able to ask questions such as:

- Does this person embrace my dreams, visions and goals?
- Are their dreams, visions and goals compatible to my lifestyle?
- Is this person a firm believer in the word of God and is this being demonstrated in their lifestyle and character?

If you don't set a standard for yourself, it is easy to allow anyone to slip through. There's a famous saying. 'If you don't stand for something you'll fall for anything'. Ask leaders, mentors and those close to you to help you identify the needs and qualities that a prospective partner ought to require. They should take into account the type of person you are and the lifestyle you live. Knowing what you want is difficult if you don't know who you are.

Know who you are
You cannot know someone else for who they are if you don't know who you are. To know who you are in Christ requires a firm foundation in Him and His word. Your relationship with God determines your effectiveness in a loving relationship with a person, as He is the ultimate guidance to a fulfilling relationship with others.

Be patient

Learning to be patient when your emotions are telling you otherwise is one of the hardest challenges for most. Patience is key. Rushing into a relationship can be damaging. Remember our formula that reads:

The wrong relationship + wrong timing = Disaster
The wrong relationship + good timing = Mistake
The right relationship + wrong timing = Hurt
The right relationship + good timing = SUCCESS!

If you are in a rush to enter into a relationship, you have to question what is the driving force behind you. Are you worried that the person may change their mind later on down the line if you remain friends? If so these kinds of insecurities will only take their toll on the relationship. Is it the rush to fulfil a hormonal desire? If so it could be lust not love. Be true to yourself, the devil is a liar, not you. You'll only hurt yourself and those involved if you are not able to truly question what may be pushing you to rush into entering a relationship, which perhaps could be better off in time. Remember there is a time for everything, (Ecclesiastes 3).

Seek Counsel

When two people are close, it is very easy to make decisions based on emotion, this may seem logical and understandable to you, but it may not always be the case. I have come across many people who admit that they find it hard to hear God's voice on the issue of a relationship because of their clouding emotions. Always involve close friends, leaders or someone who you can be accountable to, someone who has "been down the road" when it comes to the area of relationships. They are the windows to your situation. We all have blind spots we cannot see ourselves, and that is where these people will be helpful in advising you best while considering your current position. Proverbs 11:14 says: 'Where there is no counsel, the people fall; but in the multitude of counsellors there is safety'. Solomon was the wisest man to have lived, and even he believed in the saying that 'no man is an island'. Involve others.

The Benchmark:

Men
Psalm 112 is one of my favourite chapters in the bible and an ideal benchmark for every man. Let us look at this in some detail:

> *¹Praise the LORD!*
> *Blessed is the man who fears the LORD,*
> *Who delights greatly in His commandments*

The blessed man fears the Lord, because this is the beginning of wisdom and knowledge, which every man needs in order to build a successful relationship. The man in which the psalmist refers to delights in His commandments and takes pleasure in walking right with God and the law of the land. This reveals to us where his priorities in life are, and that they are set in order.

> *²His descendants will be mighty on earth;*
> *The generation of the upright will be blessed.*

He will raise great children and leaders because he himself is noble and a leader respected and looked up to by peers. He endeavours to affect his generation for the best. He becomes recognised by government, and in a modern context, society and communities, elders and leaders.

> *³Wealth and riches will be in his house,*
> *And his righteousness endures forever.*

He will obtain God given wealth and riches for his household because he puts God first.

⁴ Unto the upright there arises light in the darkness;
He is gracious, and full of compassion, and righteous.

He is a light in the midst of a dark world. He stands out. He possesses characteristics such as grace, compassion and righteousness, which are key for relationships.

⁵A good man deals graciously and lends;
He will guide his affairs with discretion.

He conducts his business and affairs in the right manner. That is to say he is just, fair, not proud or boastful, but rather humble and discrete. God guides his affairs.

⁶Surely he will never be shaken;
The righteous will be in everlasting remembrance.

God will remember him in all his matters because of their close relationship. Therefore he will not be shaken but determined and faithful.

⁷He will not be afraid of evil tidings;
His heart is steadfast, trusting in the LORD.
⁸His heart is established;
He will not be afraid,
Until he sees his desire upon his enemies.

He trusts in the Lord, despite the evil going on around him even if it's on his doorstep. He understands that the race is not to the swift and with this, remains steadfast at heart, trusting God.

⁹He has dispersed abroad,
He has given to the poor;
His righteousness endures forever;
His horn will be exalted with honour.

His descendants and dealings go beyond his circle of influence and abroad to different cultures and emerging generations. He is charitable to compliment a charitable female such as the Proverbs 31 woman who we shall touch upon later in the book. He is as mentioned righteous, not given to drunkenness, idleness, or possessiveness. He doesn't sleep around and boast in worldly activities and material things.

¹⁰The wicked will see it and be grieved;
He will gnash his teeth and melt away;
The desire of the wicked shall perish.

The wicked hate him, he faces attack for being Godly, which leads people at times to believe he's ungodly, though this is not so. He always comes through trials and tests because he is a friend of God and has God fighting his battles, his enemies perish!

The Proverbs 31 woman:

Women
What do we know about the famous Proverbs 31? The chapter consists of thirty-one verses. The first nine verses are in reference to King Lemuel. Some scholars suggest that he was an Egyptian king who in this scripture we come across only once in the bible. There is an opinion that Lemuel is actually King Solomon and that Lemuel was a fond name by which his mother referred to him. The first nine verses of Proverbs 31 are a stark warning from a mother to her son. The description of the virtuous woman

that follows is designed to show us what wives and women should aspire to be. It also indicates what a man should look for in a wife.

Proverbs 31 refers to a woman who is married, and is a virtuous wife. It is famously used as the benchmark for Christian women to aim for. However we shall consider the Proverb in regards to a relationship and will pick out key verses to see how we can adapt these principles accordingly to women who are either in relationships today or are preparing for a relationship in the future.

> *Proverbs 31:*
> *[10] Who can find a virtuous wife?*
> *For her worth is far above rubies.*

A virtuous woman means a woman of strength. Strength by wisdom, grace and the fear of the Lord. A virtuous woman has the command of her spirit and knows how to manage others. In other words she is whole and understands herself. She knows how to manage her relationships with other females who may walk in jealousy, gossip or competition against her and those around her. She's of good resolution, has good principles, and is firm and steady in her ways. She doesn't compromise to sin. The verse notes that it is hard to find such a woman, which means that if a man finds her it is likely he will treat the lady more precious than rubies and do everything to hold on to her. In order to be treated this way a young lady has to display the characteristics of a virtuous young lady. Ruth was given this title, and if you read the book of Ruth carefully you can see how Boaz picks her out and treats her accordingly.

> *[11] The heart of her husband safely trusts her;*
> *So he will have no lack of gain.*
> *[12] She does him good and not evil*

All the days of her life.
¹³She seeks wool and flax,
And willingly works with her hands.
¹⁴She is like the merchant ships,
She brings her food from afar.
¹⁵ She also rises while it is yet night,
And provides food for her household,
And a portion for her maidservants.

She is industrious and builds her husband's esteem. If a young lady wants to become a virtuous wife she ought to begin with that which she can do within the confines of a relationship. In the Proverb the woman builds her man's esteem by valuing him and letting him know how important he is. She demonstrates due affection. Affection is not just physical but emotional also and a man's esteem can vary in levels depending on what his woman says to him. She conducts herself in a way that allows him to be entirely confident in her and to not worry about her behaviour when left alone with family and friends. He trusts her completely based on her character and conduct. Some scholars interpret this verse to mean 'He trusts her chastity'. He is happy to have her and therefore does not envy those who are rich. His wife (and for our case partner) is enough. He doesn't have to look elsewhere. He is satisfied.

I thoroughly enjoy the interpretation of these verses. Some interpretations and commentaries say that the virtuous woman has studied how to love her man! Wow! Not by foolishness or fondness, but by words and esteeming. She knows not to flatter but knows the words to build him up when he's ill or down and is able to distinguish when to use humour and when to be serious. Verse 12 says she does him good all the days of her life. Even when the chips are down she maintains the same love, reverence and character towards him.

Verse 15 shows us that a virtuous woman prays through the night for her husband and their relationship. She is not out late partying and with friends; when she knows she's got business to attend to with God and her relationship, and strikes a fine balance in this respect. She doesn't sleep late and wake up late, but is bright, early and consistent in her relationship with God.

Verse 16 goes on to mention that she considers a field and then buys from her profit. What struck me reading this verse is that it reveals to us that the virtuous woman had made it her duty not to be indecisive but stable, and whole to make sound decisions, considering her family whilst doing so. The verse tells us that she buys from her profit, which indicates that she has previously been successful in that which she laid her hands on to do in the past; in order to decide and purchase in profit. Profit equals successful business, dealings and or gain.

> *17She girds herself with strength,*
> *And strengthens her arms.*

This doesn't mean she goes to the gym to pump weights. This means that she prepares herself to embrace her man's weaknesses, struggles, and challenges. She is there as a safe haven and place of comfort for him to confide in. Holding up a man spiritually is not easy so she strengthens herself in prayer to God. This is in order to strengthen herself to be able to bear the weight and burden her man may carry at times and lift him up before God.

> *20 She extends her hand to the poor,*
> *Yes, she reaches out her hands to the needy.*

She is charitable in order to compliment her 'charitable Psalm 112 man!' She does not think about her own well-being alone. She's unselfish in helping others (out of her experiences) and that which she has internally and externally to give, she consistently does with no intention to gain in return.

> [23]*Her husband is known in the gates,*
> *When he sits among the elders of the land.*

Her man is known and this is because of her efforts behind closed doors. She takes care of him, and others recognise he has a gift in his female companion.

> [25]*Strength and honour are her clothing;*
> *She shall rejoice in time to come.*

She dresses in a way, which shows her strength. She doesn't dress to impress out of insecurity and to attract others only to her physical appearance. This is because she is confident in who she is and what she can bring to a relationship and to her man. She is more than eyeliner, thighs, and pretty looks alone!

> [26] *She opens her mouth with wisdom,*
> *And on her tongue is the law of kindness.*

In other words, her talk is not idle. She talks sense naturally, and kindness is always in her mouth as if it were a strict law to her. That's because her strength is in wisdom, as we read in verse 10 of Proverbs 31.

> [29] *" Many daughters have done well,*
> *But you excel them all."*
> [30] *Charm is deceitful and beauty is passing,*
> *But a woman who fears the LORD, she shall be praised.*

She stands out for that which is in her heart, character and spirit. She may well take care of external matters but this is only a reflection of her internal order. She fears the Lord and puts Him first in her dealings towards everything that includes her relationships, thoughts and feelings.

9. HOW FAR IS TOO FAR?
(LOOKING AT PHYSICAL INTIMACY BEFORE MARRIAGE...)

Intimacy

Intimacy is more than physical contact. It includes spiritual as well as emotional feelings and can be conveyed by words, feelings and through special moments. However Christians everywhere today struggle with remaining chaste during the dating and courting stage of their relationship. It is fair to say that God made us as beings that possess sexual drives, and can understand the frustrations that come with being patient, even with good motives. However it is key that before a relationship you set your boundaries and discuss them with the person you eventually embark on a relationship with. Here are some guidelines to help you:

How far is too far?

Masturbating

Masturbation is not an answer to self-control. It is not possible to masturbate without having had a sexual thought implanted in your mind at that point or sometime prior. We must also understand that sex is not about self-fulfilment, but fulfilling the needs of your partner. It is when a married couple bear this in mind that they are able to fulfil the needs of their partner whilst having their own needs met. So if sex is not about self-fulfilment, then masturbation is not the ideal way to achieve pleasure or sexual release that God intends for an individual.

Oral sex, mutual masturbation, and intense fondling
Many will argue that there is no direct teaching on what is permissible with regard to intimacy outside of marriage. You may find that those who strongly contest this usually struggle with self-control and issues of the flesh and are looking for a license to act accordingly. Let us take a look at the following scripture from Galatians:

> *16 I say then: Walk in the Spirit, and you shall not fulfil the lust of the flesh. 17 For the flesh lusts against the Spirit, and the Spirit against the flesh; and these are contrary to one another, so that you do not do the things that you wish. 18 But if you are led by the Spirit, you are not under the law.*

The flesh pushes us towards doing that which we do not wish for ourselves; these include acts such as fornication. However verse 16 shows us that if we are led by the Spirit we will not fulfil the desires of the flesh which war against the Spirit. This means that every time an act of fornication or sin is committed it is because the flesh got the better of the parties involved:

> *James 1:*
> *13 Let no one say when he is tempted, "I am tempted by God"; for God cannot be tempted by evil, nor does He Himself tempt anyone. 14 But each one is tempted when he is drawn away by his own desires and enticed.*

15 Then, when desire has conceived, it gives birth to sin; and sin, when it is full-grown, brings forth death.

So God does not tempt man into the works of the flesh, which according to Galatians 5 are as follows:

19Now the works of the flesh are evident, which are: adultery, fornication, uncleanness, lewdness, 20idolatry, sorcery, hatred, contentions, jealousies, outbursts of wrath, selfish ambitions, dissensions, heresies, 21envy, murders, drunkenness, revelries, and the like; of which I tell you beforehand, just as I also told you in time past, that those who practice such things will not inherit the kingdom of God.

We must then understand that God is not pleased with anything that draws you and tempts you away from Him towards the flesh and the works of the flesh:

James 4:7-8
7Therefore submit to God. Resist the devil and he will flee from you. 8Draw near to God and He will draw near to you...

Acts such as oral sex, mutual masturbation, and intense fondling all come about through a process. It starts with kissing, which leads to fondling, the undressing and then further acts. The process takes you from the spirit, stage by stage to the flesh where you are no longer under the control of the spirit, and are therefore led by the flesh.

Galatians 6:22-26
22But the fruit of the Spirit is love, joy, peace, longsuffering, kindness, goodness, faithfulness, 23gentleness, self-control. Against such there is no law.

24And those who are Christ's have crucified the flesh with its passions and desires. 25If we live in the Spirit, let us also walk in the Spirit. 26Let us not become conceited, provoking one another, envying one another.

These acts provoke the parties involved to go further each time and end up becoming habitual, as do most sexual acts. Therefore in setting boundaries it is a good idea to discuss, in an honest setting with your partner, that which provokes you to the level that convicts you in the Spirit as an act of the flesh. Continuing in such acts can lead to the grieving of the Spirit where you can't even hear God's voice any more because you're so drawn away with the flesh. Sex is for marriage not for the person you hope to marry, there is a difference.

Crucifying the flesh and its desires takes time and commitment from both parties. If you find yourself in sexual sin or in a relationship where you feel the intimacy is not Godly, there needs to be a commitment to crucify the flesh. You need to put boundaries up and pray together through the physical temptation and desire that comes as a consequence of this discipline. If this is not the case one may end up bitter and withdrawn. If your partner wants to fulfil the desires of the flesh despite knowing it's wrong you need to review your relationship. Such acts remove the ability to talk and grow together spiritually and emotionally. It is also commonly known that physical intimacy can overlook relational flaws, which in turn will destroy the relationship. Talking to one another, and allowing the Spirit's conviction is key. Avoiding tempting situations is also important:

1 Thessalonians 5:
19 Do not quench the Spirit. 21 Test all things; hold fast what is good. 22 Abstain from every form of evil.

Ephesians 5:3
³ But fornication and all uncleanness or covetousness, let it not even be named among you, as is fitting for saints;

1 Corinthians 6:18
¹⁸ Flee sexual immorality. Every sin that a man does is outside the body, but he who commits sexual immorality sins against his own body.

Seeking help

If you struggle with any of the aforementioned acts seek Godly counsel on the matter. Pray for God's help and self control, that you may walk in the Spirit and not the flesh. Ask Him for the boldness to confide in someone else. The enemy will want you to keep your issues to yourself and will do all he can to put you down. However God is merciful and just to forgive you. And if you and your partner struggle with this issue then praying and seeking counsel is ideal. Blaming each other for the sexual desires God created you with is not the answer. You are a team. Protect your relationship and know that your confidentiality is secure in one another.

Psalm 1:1
¹Blessed is the man
Who walks not in the counsel of the ungodly,

The worldly view of sex differs greatly to God's view on sex, so seeking worldly help will be of no use.

10.UNDERSTANDING MALE AND FEMALE COMMUNICATION, DIFFERENCES AND NEEDS

Male and female differences and needs:
Before entering into a relationship it is worth having a brief look at the differences and needs between men and women. This can prove to be a useful insight. The following are just a number of points presented as result of research undertaken by Willard F Harley in his book 'His needs Her needs'. [1] Let's explore these items a little further:

The needs of a Woman:
- Affection
- Communication
- Honesty & Openness
- Security

The needs of a Man:
- Admiration
- An attractive partner
- Domestic Security
- Recreational Companionship

1: His Needs Her Needs: Building an affair proof marriage by Willard F Harley

Needs of a woman:

Affection

Willard Harley's research makes us aware of just how important affection can be to a woman. He suggests that affection is a symbol of protection, security, and approval, and concludes that they are all important to women. Signs of outward affection display the concern for, and the importance of, a woman to her partner. With this in mind I suggest that when one is strongly considering starting a relationship that they spend time discussing what their understanding of affection is and how they would like this to be communicated. This allows a person to find out what their partner understands as affection and they can agree on ways in which this can be communicated.

Communication

Women tend to want communication from their partner. This is someone who they can talk to and someone that can talk to their spirit and to their heart. Someone she can converse with both intellectually and with humour. Some men may openly admit they find it hard to communicate or express themselves verbally, however women tend to feel that open and honest verbal conversation is an important need in their relationship.

Honesty & Openness

Sometimes men may tend to find it hard to express what they might be thinking or feeling. This is not always intentional but may sometimes take root in their logical way of thinking. While a woman may want her partner to be expressive, men often attempt to figure things out alone. As a result some women may feel disappointed by this. Women tend to want their partner to learn to express what they are feeling. It is important to them to build an emotional connection. Men may tend to misunderstand the importance of constant honest communication that women require. This is because often for a woman to feel secure they need an understanding of a man's past, present and even future. This includes what he has previously achieved and what he is out on a mission to accomplish. It is important for men reading this to understand this, as such information is what women tend to use as a foundation to build intimate solid relationships with their partner and to grow closer to them.

Security

When a woman doesn't feel comfortable in a man's environment it could be because the man has not proved himself responsible or trustworthy to her. In order for a female to be in a position where she feels she can be expressive she has to feel secure and comfortable. This also refers to the emotional security that her man provides for her, as well as general security for her well-being. Willard Harley in his book 'His needs Her needs' suggests that though a woman may not marry a man for his money, she does want him to have enough money to support her. Women tend to want financial security from a man, a man who brings the financial arrangements to the table.

Needs of a Man:

Admiration

Prior to writing this book, I had heard from a number of men that the more their partner esteems them, the more they feel like a "king" and want to treat their woman accordingly as their due "queen" . These same men also admitted that while any female may congratulate them on an achievement, the sense of worth couldn't be measured to that of their partner's compliments.

A man wants to be admired by his woman, and women should bear in mind that there is a child in every man! There is a superman who wants to be someone's hero, and wants their partner to be their biggest fan.

An attractive partner

One thing throughout the book we have discussed is the importance of looking at the internal characteristics of a person and not being drawn to the external and physical appearance alone. It is fair to note that usually the initial attraction of a man to a woman is physical, before he decides whether to take it further by getting to know her. It is this form of attraction that is so primary for a man. It may not be true of all cases but certainly in many, if not the majority. A woman who enters a relationship should bear this in mind as it is often stated that men tend to want a woman who avoids complacency in their appearance once they have entered into a relationship.

Domestic Security

According to Harley, today men are faced with the pressures of work, family and what society deem a man's role in the world to be. This alone is a good reason for a man to want domestic security. In relating this to relationships it suggests that finding out how to support a man with his goals, ambitions, work, and studies goes a long way in a man's heart. Harley further argues that being able to help a man achieve such whilst making it a pleasurable engagement, (and what I would also add as creative) speaks volumes of a woman's support to her partner.

Recreational Companionship

A man may tend to want to share his most exciting times not with friends alone, but with the one he cherishes and loves. Harley once again suggests that taking an interest in a man's pursuits and hobbies and to share these moments would ultimately mean the world to him. Doing such can build a close companionship for a couple. Especially as Harley suggests that a man's partner should also be his best friend.

Male and Female communication styles:

Dr Roger Sperry won a noble peace prize in 1989 for his studies on medicine and the human brain [2]. He discovered that in the sixteenth

2: Ray Mossholder, Marriage Plus (Lake Mary, FL: Charisma House, 1990)

week of gestation there is a chemical reaction that takes place on the right side of a man's brain that doesn't take place in a female's brain. As a result of this chemical reaction he concluded that men tend to be more logical in their way of thinking while women are often led by their emotions.

As a result some men tend to have difficulty expressing their emotions in particular situations. They tend to take more time to think things over and to express themselves verbally. When faced with challenges they often keep quiet to avoid distractions that may take their thinking from A to C, when they want to keep it a straightforward A to B. This doesn't mean that men are not emotional. It is such thinking which makes it harder for men to open up and become vulnerable in relationships. Allowing room for a man to think in this manner and in helping him express his thoughts where necessary and may be useful especially in instances such as a major disagreement.

Here's an example to illustrate our ways of thinking. If you ask a female how her day went you may get an answer such as:

"My day was fine! I met up with Marie and we went shopping. When we went shopping we met this cute guy who helped us find our way. When we got there this guy showed us where to go and we got these lovely shoes on discount."...And she may continue.

However at this point the guy would probably be thinking, "All I asked was how was your day!" And so in asking the guy the same question you are most likely to get a response along the lines of:

"It was fine thanks".

A man's response may be simple and straightforward leaving the woman to ponder on how he could describe the day's events in four words. In understanding that such differences have occurred from birth, we don't concur on these differences but rather use this as a basis of understanding when relating to the opposite sex without jumping to conclusions. Such differences cause us to learn patience in relating to one another in every aspect of communication in our relationships and help us in our communication with one another.

Conflict Styles
Here are five styles that we can look at to help us understand how we communicate with the opposite sex during times of conflict.

Yield
Someone who yields is someone who for the sake of the relationship doesn't want to make a fuss during times of conflict. They are hugely concerned for the relationship but rarely have their needs met, as they tend to keep quiet and are reluctant in expressing their true feelings. This is because they want to keep their partner happy and fear that disagreements may ultimately lead to a split. As a result they tend to keep most of their frustrations within themselves, which only does their partner and themselves further emotional damage and does not benefit the relationship at all.

Withdraw
One who withdraws during conflict may walk away from a heated discussion, or hang up the phone in frustration or anger. Alternatively they may not outwardly display those actions but withdraw instead becoming desensitised to their partner and their plea for reconciliation by closing up emotionally. Acts may include bouts of silence, or refusing to talk. They don't appear to have a concern for the relationship during times of conflict but this doesn't always reflect their value of the

relationship as a whole. However they often find that their needs are not met in their relationship, as they never get around to expressing how they truly felt as a result of withdrawing during conflict.

Self-centred

The self-centred view of conflict resolution is when one is only concerned with their needs being met, and feel that they are always right. Everything must be the way they desire or they may throw a tantrum. If they want to talk about something immediately, it must be done there and then, regardless of what you may have ahead of you. Such individuals have their needs met, but it is out of selfish desires. They are not really taking the needs and cares of their partner into account and as a result, though their needs are being met, they have no concern for the relationship. Individuals who behave as such during conflict tend to be unaware at most times of their position unless identified by a third party. Where this is failed to be noted in a relationship it may lead to a relationship split at the surprise of that individual.

Resolve

The resolution style of conflict is what we should all aim for during times of difficulty and conflict in relationships. The resolution conflict style is where individuals have a high concern for the relationship and for their partner. Where a couple both display such actions, it reveals their love and regard for one another. Their relationship is of high concern and so they are open with one another in order to meet each other's needs and understand each other's point of view. They are willing to listen, understand and settle conflict for the peace of the relationship and out of genuine love. They have boundaries to their conflicts and have established rules on conflict resolution. This is where we should all aim to be in regards to conflict in every aspect of our relationships with people.

Compromise

Someone who compromises may vary between the conflict styles previously mentioned. They may for example either withdraw if they find themselves in conflict at a time when they are emotionally or physically tired. They may yield at a time when they feel they need to have their partner's love and support, and as a result, want to avoid the worse case scenario. They may display acts of selfishness in order for things to work according to their desires, or they may look to resolve in order to promote a positive and helpful way of communicating during conflict.

Summary

Be honest with yourself, and re-evaluate the various different conflict styles, see if you can identify which style or styles you tend to adopt in the heat of conflict. Perhaps you are someone who often tends to yield for the sake of keeping peace in your relationship, but as a result are not truly happy in that relationship. Perhaps you are someone who withdraws and needs to consider how withdrawing in conflict affects both you and your partner. Maybe you are someone who doesn't yield or withdraw but on reflection of these styles now understands that you could be less self-centred and more considerate of your partner's desires. Whatever the case, if you can identify a conflict style then discussing these styles with your partner, and reviewing them in your mind at the point of conflict with a view to achieving the resolution style of conflict is what we all ought to set out to achieve.

11. SEVERING OLD TIES...

Severing old ties

Entering into a relationship off the back of a bad relationship, on the rebound or in search of having the wrong needs met is clearly wrong. We can refer to such people as individuals who bring baggage into relationships. A very well known source of baggage is that of an ungodly soul tie.

> *1 Samuel 18:*
> *[1] Now when he had finished speaking to Saul, the soul of Jonathan was knit to the soul of David, and Jonathan loved him as his own soul.*

Some versions say that Jonathan's soul became one with that of David. The New King James Version uses the term 'knit'.

The meaning of knit is to loop and entwine. This is what happens when one has a soul tie and two become one. There are Godly soul ties and ungodly soul ties. That of Jonathan and David was Godly. The bible tells us that he loved him as his own soul. If you read on in the book of Samuel you will see that as Saul seeks to take David's life, Saul's own son Jonathan goes against his father's secrecy to protect David, and is reduced to tears when David has to flee. For Jonathan to go against his own family and weep beacuse of seperation between him and David shows us just how close they were.

We as humans have a body, a spirit and a soul. In our soul we have three key components that make up the soul realm. They are:

- Our emotions – feelings
- Our will   – decisions and choices we make
- Our mind   – our thoughts – that which we think.

There are also various levels of closeness and intimacy that we have with people that we need to look at. They are broken into four groups:

Acquaintance
The basic level, where you occasionally talk to someone but know little about that person. This could be a fellow colleague, worker or student for example.

Casual
This is where you share common interests with these people and meet in more personal contexts. For an example as a minister I meet artists with whom I relate to on a ministry level. We see each other at various events where we have been invited to minister or attend in person. Outside these realms I am unaware of what their lifestyle consists of.

Level of closeness & fellowship
This is where you share common interests, ideas and goals with this person and enjoy each other's company, even meeting from time to

time. You help each other and are there for one another. For example a close friend or someone at church.

Extremely Intimate

This is the level where you spend a lot of time together, communicate honestly on a regular basis, and feel free around each other. This is the level at which soul ties are created. 'How?' you may ask. Well let's examine a little further. We as human beings are unlikely to associate with people who put us down or don't agree with our spirit. Therefore you'll find out that the people you spend the most of your recreational time with are those who you deem close. In order for us to communicate at a deep and intimate level with someone we usually want to know that the person is trustworthy. Knowing this allows you to confide in the person but also leaves you vulnerable.

Severing old ties

Because we don't like having our vulnerability and weaknesses exposed we confide in those who are close to us, and hence give them a piece of our heart and or soul. You do not speak or act freely around everyone, but those who are close to you and accept you for who you are. With these people you've often got nothing to prove or hide. It's with such friendships that you tend to use your money to buy gifts and make things happen, such as going on dinner outings for example. When you engage in a level of closeness as such with someone of the opposite sex who also on top of this appeals to you, you become more friendly, and gradually become attached to the extent that not hearing from him or her after a short period of time is no longer a normal thing. Some become so attached that they must see or speak to this person everyday. This is a soul tie, and like David and Jonathan it doesn't require sex to form but the transferring of the three key elements which make up the soul. It is your emotions that tell you, that you can't go on without speaking to that person for one day though you may not even be together in a relationship.

It is your decision to make time for someone, and it is your choice of whom you allow to get close to you. It is dangerous to allow anyone to come up to this level of acquaintance and closeness, without testing their character and motives for such. In addition to this, some people not only give away their soul, but they give away their spirit and body.

In other words they give themselves away when they have sex with someone outside marriage. One afternoon the Holy Spirit opened my eyes to a wonderful revelation. He asked me as I stood meditating on the word in my kitchen 'Where does worship take place?' I replied "In the church". The conversation was not a verbal one, but the revelation was a step-by-step process at the speed and response of a verbal conversation with a human being. Having answered, the Holy Spirit asked me again where worship takes place, challenging me to think even deeper.

You see the church is not the building it's the people. With this in mind, and understanding that worship is a lifestyle, I was able to respond to the Holy Spirit by saying that worship takes place in the temple. As Christians, our body is the temple of the Holy Spirit:

> 1 Corinthians 6:
> [19]Or do you not know that your body is the temple of the Holy Spirit who is in you, whom you have from God,

It has been the objective of the enemy lucifer to have people worship him. This resulted in him being thrown out of heaven, but he still wants people to worship him, and attempts to get this worship in the subtlest ways such as music for an example. With this, the devil is happy every time a believer commits fornication, especially with an unsaved person. The word of God says:

2 Corinthians 6:
[14] Do not be unequally yoked together with unbelievers. For what fellowship has righteousness with lawlessness? And what communion has light with darkness?

Unbelievers are in the darkness; it is those who have found Christ that are in the light. So when there is sin or someone becomes 'one' in a relationship or through having sex with an unbeliever, it gives satan an opportunity to pollute a believer's soul. Sex is more than the physical, it is also spiritual. Have you ever seen a married couple that grow together in marriage and end up looking alike? That's because spirits are exchanged. I once spoke to an unbeliever who approached me for counselling regarding her anger. She complained that from seemingly no where she had outbursts of anger that she didn't know were in her. I asked her if she was seeing anyone. She told me she was, and I questioned whether they were sexually active. She said they were, and very much so too. I asked her if her boyfriend struggled with anger and self-restraint. It appeared to be the case to such a bad degree. With this information alone I was able to convince this unbeliever about the concept of soul ties and even she was able to accept that she had exchanged such traits in becoming one with this person. When the enemy corrupts a person's spirit (by exchanging dark spirits as they merge sexually and become one) the soul tie and bondage intensifies. That's why we have unfortunate cases of young ladies who despite being physically abused by their partners still return to them and engage in sexual activities with them. It's not because they enjoy being physically abused but because their soul is tied and they are drawn to that person. When a Christian is drawn to a wrong spirit they find it hard to break off, to the extent that some give up altogether by continuing to give in to a person sexually and even backslide. Maybe you can identify with this and realise that this will hold you back from a new and Godly relationship, if so then it's important that we look at how someone can break free from a soul tie. In addition to this your extremes may not be as such, yet there may be a lack of peace in your heart about the relationship. Here are some steps you can take to break free from an ungodly soul tie and or relationship:

Confession
The first step to freedom is acknowledgement. Acknowledging that you have an emotional and or physical soul tie is an open honest sign before God that you want to be free. Secondly, you must maintain that honesty by renouncing the name or names of those people you want to be set free from, naming the sin specifically.

Healing
Ask God to forgive you from the bitterness of past mistakes, failures and experiences. Ask God to wash you afresh and anew, and bring that which you want to be removed to the surface in order for you to deal with those issues. This may be a painful process, which may lead you to become emotional if done in true reverence and sincerity.

Objects
Remove all objects such as items of jewellery you may be wearing that remind you or take you back to those thoughts.

Counsel
Ask your leader, mentors, close friends, and family to pray with you and even fast on your behalf for deliverance, as well as being there for you as a listening ear.

Decide
Decide to flee all appearances of evil, which may take you back to a stage of bondage and put yourself in a Godly environment with Godly people who will stand by you.

Healing may take time. It requires patience, and you may have to go through the motions. However be persistent and God will see you through!

The last chapter of this book takes a biblical story and relates it to lessons we can learn and apply to our lives today. It's a story I wrote of a message I preached at the annual (Jesus For Life Youth Ministry) J4L True Love event. It's a timely story, which I pray will bless you!

12. TRUE LOVE
(THE STORY BEHIND THE MESSAGE)

True love

Love is defined according to the Collins dictionary as "having a passionate desire, longing, feelings for, attachment to and affection for. To desire or like something very much. An intense emotion of affection, warmth, fondness, and regard towards someone or something". It is also described as a "whole hearted liking or pleasure in something".

In the Bible, the apostle Paul describes love as longsuffering, kind, not envious, not "puffed up". He describes love as "something that does not behave rudely, which is not provoked or seeks itself". Paul goes on to describe that love does not "fail or rejoice in iniquity but rejoices in truth". (1 Corinthians 13:1-8 paraphrased).

There are four types of love namely, Eros, Storgé, Phillia and Agape. We need to take a brief look at each one in order to discover what true and genuine love is and where true love lives.

The first type of love that is commonly known is taken from the Greek word:

Eros
This is the type of love found between married couples, the romantic love as described in the book of Song of Solomon. This is where we get the English word "erotic".

Secondly there is the family type of love known as:

Storgé
This is the love found between families, brothers and sisters, mother and son, father and daughter. This is the fondness that is found between relatives.

Thirdly there is:

Philia
This is affectionate love. The word 'Philia' is found in the U.S. city Philadelphia, which is known as the city of brotherly love, and is taken from the book of Revelation Chapter 3. This type of love reflects a spontaneous warm-hearted and affectionate love. It refers to the liking and attractive appeal of friendship and is also found between the closest of friends.

Then there's the Agape love.

Agape
This is the love of choice. Many Christians are familiar with the word Agape. It can often be misunderstood because Agape love can be referred to as divine love. This can be misunderstood as love from God to man and vice-versa. However Agape love is the love commanded by God to one another regardless of their age, race or gender.

It's a love towards those around you and not those who you single out to love. It is the love that even when a person doesn't appeal to us in anyway shape or form, they are still accepted and treated well. Agape love is the love that covers sins and encourages people to treat others with respect. It builds one another up. This is the type of love that is described in 1 Corinthians 13.

Samson found himself attracted to a Philistine woman in Judges 14. He was attracted to her and in his delight decided to tell his parents all about her. His parents were not impressed, and questioned why he had chosen a heathen, and desired to marry outside of their culture. In a modern day context this could be likened to a believer marrying an unbeliever (2 Corinthians 6:14-15). In Judges 14 Samson marries this same Philistine woman.

Samson posed a riddle to the people of her town Timnah, and they struggled to resolve it. Unaware to Samson's knowledge, the people of her town had threatened his wife to get the answer out of her husband for them. Rather than tell Samson, she began to throw emotional tantrums claiming that if Samson 'really loved her' he would tell her. Samson had not told his parents yet, but she persisted in her questioning for days to the point where Samson got fed up and told her the answer to the riddle. Samson's wife shares the answer with the people of the town who were then able to present him with a solution to the riddle he proposed for them. Not to be undone, of course, Samson was well aware that they had prised their answer from his wife and this infuriated him. He decided to go back to his father's house and his wife was given to his best friend according to Judges 14:20.

The plot thickens as Samson was not made aware of these circumstances until he visits his wife a short while afterwards (Judges 15). He wanted to see his wife but his father-in-law did not permit him. He told Samson that he gave his wife away thinking that Samson hated her and didn't want to see her again. In his renewed anger Samson killed at least a thousand men with the jawbone of a donkey. The story doesn't end there. In fact it only gets more interesting. Samson was grieved and ends up going to Gaza where he meets and sleeps with a harlot. How easy is it to search for love when you thought a true-found love was present in your life?

How easy is it to be on the rebound after that broken relationship that people can find themselves sleeping around or with someone they really ought not to be with? This was the case with Samson. In Gaza the Gazites heard that Samson was in town, he wasn't much liked. After a while Samson met Delilah, who he loved, this is the third woman we come across in this story. Note that Judges 16:4 tells us that he loved Delilah. After having lost a true love to his best friend, having slept with a prostitute, Samson found himself in love again, albeit with the wrong person.

I believe it was easy for Samson to fall in love with the wrong person due to previous experiences. He loved Delilah. (Delilah means lustful). The lords of the Philistines knew something was going on between Samson and Delilah. They wanted revenge for the damage he had previously caused and instructed Delilah to entice him. Not that, this would be hard for a lustful individual. They instructed her to entice him and find out where his strength was, in order that they might overpower him and afflict him (Judges 16:5). Similar to the betrayal of Jesus by Judas, with money involved, Delilah was offered eleven hundred pieces of silver to do this.

Now you know why the scripture in 1 Timothy 6:10 tells us that the love of money is the root of all kinds of evil. Delilah acts by asking Samson where his strength lies. Each time he gave an answer he found himself having to tackle the Philistines who waited on a signal to go in and attack. What amazes me is that Samson lied to Delilah about where his strength really lay on four separate occasions, and didn't even figure out the fact that every time he told her, he found himself in a position in which he had to ward off Philistines.

He should have questioned Delilah's insistence on knowing his weakness and why he found himself up against the Philistines each time he enlightened her. But guess what? They say love blinds. That's why people continually find themselves in an abusive relationship. Their souls are tied to the person. They are either blinded to reality by what they call 'love' or are fully aware of what is going on but cannot tear themselves away for fear of being hurt. This was the unfortunate case of Samson. Delilah pulled that famous old line that Samson originally heard from his first wife and first love 'How can you say you love me when your heart is not with me?' (Judges 16:15).

She didn't just take his heart; she took his life in the end. We are warned in Proverbs 7:27 not to be led down that path as this only leads to the grave.

Delilah according to the scripture in Judges 16:16 pestered him daily with her words and pressed him until his soul was vexed to death! Someone he loved pressed him to death for money, lulling him to sleep. He was taken captive after he confessed his heart to her. If you continue reading this amazing story you will see how Samson died as a result, taking many to the grave with him in his discomfort (Judges 16:30). Amongst the many lessons to be learnt in this story, is the fact that true love is not found in a person or partner, in a girlfriend or boyfriend, until it is first found in the place where it lives.

Joseph had a dream in Genesis 37; and as he ought to, he shared his dream with his family. Little did he know that even his own family would be jealous and betray him. Where is the Storgé love here? Joseph was sold into slavery by his own family. Even your family can let you down. Maybe as you're reading you can identify with this. Your experience could be similar to that of Joseph or even worse experiences such as abuse or family separation.

Friends come and go; some enter our lives to see what they can get and not to offer anything. Once they have got what they want they are no longer interested in the relationship. Though we are commanded to show and live by Agape love, it is sad to say that we are living in a time where people see themselves as number one, the first and last call, and are rarely willing to listen or sacrifice anything for the sake of others.

Here's the good news. The bible says in Proverbs 18:24 that there is a friend that sticks closer than a brother. In other words though your mum, dad, and family may have let you down like Joseph's family, God won't let you down as long as you have Him in your life. Joseph had God and that's how his unfortunate circumstance of being sold into slavery and ending up in prison on false accusations led him to fulfilling his dream and becoming the second in command to the king of Egypt. That's why the scripture shows us in Romans 8:28 that all things work together for the good of those who love Christ and are called according to His purposes. However that condition and promise is for those who love Him and are called according to His purposes, not just anyone, but His faithful believers.

David said in Psalm 27:10 "When my mother and father forsake me the Lord will take care of me."

Maybe you have found yourself looking for love in the wrong places. Maybe you have been searching for it in a partner and you can relate to the story of Samson. Maybe it's in friends who have let you down and broken your trust even though they proclaimed several times to you that they were trustworthy. Maybe your family have forsaken you. The word of God says in 2nd Corinthians 6:18 that "He will be a Father to you and you shall be His sons and daughters". Maybe you're crushed by the loss of a loved one. The word of God says that God is close to those who are broken hearted and He saves such as have a contrite Spirit (Psalm 34:18).

It is only when you have found true love in Jesus Christ that you can experience true love on this earth with spouses, relatives and friends. The Word of God says in Psalm 118:8 that "it is better to trust in the Lord than have confidence in man". When you don't have Jesus in your life you have nothing to fall back on in times of trial and pain. If there is something wrong with my DVD player I take it back to the manufacturer. If there is something wrong with you, you have to go back to your Manufacturer, that is your Creator.

He made you and knows everything about you. He is waiting for a friendship with you, that he may show you the meaning of 'True Love'. This is because 'True Love' lives in Him. For the word of God tells us in 1 John 4:8 that God is love. What better way to lay down His life for His friends (1 John 3:16), than to send His one and only begotten Son Jesus Christ to die to forgive you of all your sins and mistakes (John 3: 16-17). There's nothing you have done that is too bad for Him to not love you. Now that is True Love, and True Love lives in Jesus Christ.

If you would like to sincerely experience this love and want to accept and begin a relationship or perhaps renew your relationship with Jesus Christ pray this prayer with sincerity right now. Take a minute wherever you are to say these few words:

Father in heaven,
I come to you right now acknowledging that I am a sinner.
I confess my sins before you right now (Confess your sins).
I believe that you sent your one and only son Jesus Christ, to die on the cross for me. You did this that I may have a new life and live eternally and abundantly with you.
Amen.

It's that simple in beginning a new relationship with someone who can show you what true love really means. Now you have taken that first bold step, I would like to hear from you and see how I can help you in your new found walk with Jesus Christ. If you sincerely prayed that prayer, and would like additional information and comments write to me at:

Kunlé Oyedeji Ministries
PO Box 51239
London SE17 2YE

Or visit:
www.kunleoyedeji.com
God Bless you!

Additional materials concerning relationships by Kunlé Oyedeji include:

• Sex, Relationships & Soul ties

• Growing In Relationships

• Making Love Work

For more inspirational life changing products by Kunlé Oyedeji visit: www.kunleoyedeji.com

ABOUT THE AUTHOR:

Kunlé Oyedeji is a motivational and inspirational speaker, teacher and writer. He is the founder, leader and Managing Director of Kunlé Oyedeji Ministries, Jesus For Life Youth Ministry and the Personal Development Company: Life Solutions. Crossing and breaking denominational barriers Kunlé addresses thousands through speaking invitations every year in churches, conferences, rallies, universities, schools, and businesses. As a speaker in high demand Relationship Matters comes as a result of this demand alongside the seminars and workshops Kunlé regularly hosts.

Kunlé gained his BA Honours Degree from Roehampton University in Theology & Religious Studies with Sociology & Psychology.

Affiliations

www.kunleoyedeji.com

EDUCATION ON LIFE

www.lifesolutionsweb.com

www.J4L.org

Notes:

Notes:

Notes:

Notes:

Notes: